# MARKS OF GOD

## ORDINARY LIVES TOUCHED BY GOD

GW01080795

Edited by Isabella Read

Foreword by Paul Perkin

st marks church, battersea rise

Published in 2008 by St Mark's Church, Battersea Rise, London SW11 1EJ

Copyright © St Mark's Church, Battersea Rise 2008

ISBN 978-0-9560827-0-1

# Acknowledgements

Sincere thanks to all the people who made this book possible.

The idea for this book was first suggested by Paul Perkin who has since given much guidance and advice, contributed his own testimony, written the foreword and reviewed the whole text.

The book cover was very kindly designed by Sharon Platt, a graphic designer and member of St Mark's Church. Nick Fulcher, a former member, kindly helped out with some technical advice concerning the cover.

The text was proof-read by members of the congregation: Caroline King who works in publishing and is trained to do this type of work; Lulu Wells, an English teacher; and our Children's Pastor Hayley Smith, an English graduate. Thanks also for their invaluable advice along the way whenever certain language details needed to be clarified.

Technical expertise, moral and practical support have all been tirelessly provided by Andy Read.

A balanced perspective was given by David Larlee for the afterword (entitled Exploring Further).

Last but not least, a big thank you to all the people who contributed their valuable testimonies, without which this book would not have been possible. You are all stars!

To everyone who played their part, big or small, thank you so much.

To God be the glory!

# Editor's Note

Some of the testimonies in this book are from interviews given at the sharing spot during the services at St Mark's Church, Battersea Rise. Members of staff lead the service and either conduct the interviews themselves or open the microphone to members of the congregation. The following are staff members who are mentioned in this context:

Rev. Paul Perkin
Vicar

Rev. Tim Mayfield
Assistant Minister

Rev. David Larlee
Curate

Nick Stott
Curate

# Contents

# Foreword

The testimonies of changed lives in answer to prayer are powerful and vital. They reinforce the truth of the claims of Christians that God is alive, and, through Jesus Christ, is actively transforming people's lives today. Without such reinforcement the Christian message would be less than the Good News of which the New Testament speaks. However, it has in fact been our discovery that the message is true; it is real; and it is utterly relevant to twenty-first-century questions of life.

In the lives of a congregation of people no different from thousands of other churches in Britain, as well as all over the world, Jesus is changing lives: giving us hope, convincing us of truth and meaning, releasing us from addictions, healing bodies, minds and spirits, strengthening us in difficulty, and restoring relationships. These testimonies are offered in the hope that they will bring encouragement and reassurance to go on looking for more 'Marks of God' — signs of His presence available to us in Jesus.

Paul Perkin

September 2008

# 1. Searching

Life has its ups and downs for everyone. But for Emma Edwards it got desperate. Read her powerful story of finding answers:

## Everything to Do with New Age

'I wasn't brought up in a practising Christian family. Up until four years ago I was a real hippie chick. My life was very much involved with clubbing and taking drugs at weekends. I was very much into the occult and I used to go and see lots of tarot card readers. I classified myself as very spiritual and I led my life by tarot cards, mediums, palmists, astrology — everything to do with New Age.

## Never Satisfied

'My motivation for getting involved in all of this was that I never really fitted in anywhere. I felt like a bit of an outsider. I found identity in the New Age and I thought this was who Emma was. To be honest, I come from a broken family and background, so I was searching for something. I had this big void in my life, a real emptiness. Whatever I tried to fill it with — drugs, alcohol, New Age — I was never satisfied. I was searching for happiness, joy and peace.

# Alone, Isolated and Misunderstood

'For nearly 15 years, I had a recurring nightmare that was with me most evenings. It would terrorise me at night and would leave me in real despair the following day. The impact this had on my life was very damaging. It caused me to suffer tremendous anxieties and fears.

'Over the years I sought numerous different types of therapy like counselling (seeing several counsellors) and psychotherapy. I opened up to one of my counsellors and said that what I was experiencing was real; it wasn't in my head, but that there was something happening at night that wasn't good. But she just couldn't understand. I asked the counsellor if she thought what I was saying sounded crazy. "Yes" was her answer! I felt I had been put in a box and labelled, which made me feel even more alone, isolated and misunderstood.

# Desperate

'Over the years I was so desperate, I got myself into a lot of debt trying to seek help for myself by going to different spiritual healers and mediums. I was very much into Reiki [a form of alternative healing, originating in Japan] and crystal healing because I was just searching so much for someone to help me. I was unaware at the time that this was only heightening my problems. I became even more depressed and exhausted and was struggling with life.

'Eventually I ended up seeing a psychotherapist, who had me undergo several hospital tests. I spoke to the psychotherapist, explaining that I thought the results of the tests would come back clear, as what I was experiencing was spiritual not physical. The test results did indeed come back negative! They just couldn't find what it was.

'In April 2004, I transferred to a new job and soon became aware that both my boss and my colleague were Christians. I broke down to them on quite a few occasions, telling them about the nightmares. I explained how I'd tried everything and nobody could help me. They both showed me so much compassion, support and understanding.

# 'I Don't Believe in God!'

'My boss told me about St Mark's Church, Battersea Rise, and that she felt this would be a place where I'd fit in. I can remember saying to her, "I'm not the type of person to go to church. I don't believe in God!" My impression of church was very negative. I thought it was full of old people, real Bible bashers and lots of rules and regulations, which was not how I wanted to lead my life.

'After my boss and I spoke about church, I left it for several months. Then one morning I woke up and I really was at breaking point. I didn't want to continue suffering like this anymore. I thought, *Well Emma, you've got two choices here: you either don't know what you're going to do with your life, or you try church — because if that really doesn't help then this is going to be your life and what a miserable, unhappy life you're going to have.*

# Outside St Mark's

'So I got up the courage and stood outside St Mark's. As I was writing down the Alpha Course details, I can remember clearly cringing and feeling so embarrassed thinking, *What are these people in the cars driving by thinking of me?!* I felt real shame that I had to go to church. I came to the evening service that Sunday and was overwhelmed when I walked into St Mark's. I had a real sense of peace and love.

'When I came home, something just clicked in me and I thought, *This is the place for me to be.* It felt as if I had finally come to the right place. I was surprised and encouraged to see so many young people and I was amazed to see such a modern band. It was not what I was expecting at all. I was very pleasantly surprised and my perception of church changed from that night on.

# Such Kindness

'I loved the service and then decided to do the Alpha Course which started that Wednesday. Even through the Alpha Course, I still didn't classify myself as a Christian and I continued to struggle a lot with the occult. During the course I received such kindness, understanding and acceptance, which enticed me to return each week. I did, however, struggle all the way through the course trying to understand and accept that New Age involvement could have consequences in a person's life. I can remember the leaders in my group saying to me, "It's okay, Emma, to keep your own opinions. It might be something that God will change in you at a different time." That is exactly what happened!

## 'I Could See Clearly for the First Time'

'Towards the end of the course, I opened up to my group and explained about the nightmares. One of the helpers mentioned how he and his wife would be able to help me with this and suggested I contact them when I was ready. When the time felt right, I started to meet up with this couple [David and Rachel Larlee] on a regular basis. It was so liberating to finally be amongst people who understood and believed what I was saying and experiencing. They took me through deep prayer sessions and taught me a great deal about who Jesus is and about forgiveness.

'It took a lot of time but, through prayer and God's love, the most powerful and amazing things happened through these sessions. That was the turning point and I realised, *God really is real! He is the almighty One and He has power over everything on this earth!* God opened my eyes. It was like I could see clearly for the first time. Everything I was involved in was the cause of my nightmares and it was such an amazing revelation. The spiritual experiences I had during my times with Dave and Rach were powerful and convinced me that I was able to put my trust in Jesus.

## Something Very Gentle and Personal...

'Something very gentle and personal happened between God and me. Each morning when I woke up, I felt God giving me the sense that everything I had in my bedroom to do with the occult was damaging and I needed to get rid of it. Over several months I ended up throwing everything to do with the occult away. I made a lot of sacrifices — I disconnected myself from certain people and certain therapies.

'As soon as I did that, there was real closure. God freed me from these nightmares. It was truly amazing and it didn't cost me a penny! To be able to sleep peacefully at night is such a blessing. I couldn't have done it without God. No doctor, no psychotherapist, no spiritual healer was able to free me from this; only God has the power to do it. Where I was in so much darkness, He has shone His glorious light into my heart, into my life. God has transformed me in the way I see and think, in the way I respond to people. I love my life now! He is the most important person in my life and nothing would come between us now. Praise God!'

Praise God indeed, for He is our Healer and our Deliverer!

# 2. God's Intervention

As New Wine [a Christian camping conference] 2007 approached, James Ewins gave us an updated, yet poignant, reminder of his testimony from the previous year's event:

## The Darkest and Most Difficult Time

'When I went to New Wine last year, I had had my second bout of cancer, which came just after my second child was born to me and my wife, Tiff. We were at a very low ebb because, since my diagnosis in the September of 2005, God had remained utterly silent to us for a period of about nine months. [James had felt a lack of peace and a sense of prayers being unanswered. There had been no tangible sense of God's presence in the way he had been used to.] That was the darkest and most difficult time we'd ever had.

'We turned up at New Wine exhausted, but resolute that we were going to go, because it was a goal that we wanted to achieve: that we got there. But we were very, very low. We all went along one evening to hear a speaker called David Carr. He was billed as being a little unorthodox, a bit radical and prophetic. Everyone from St Mark's went along, very excited to hear him. David Larlee reserved us some seats (because we were slightly late — having put the children to bed) and they were on the front row.

# A Broken Heart

'David Carr began to speak. He spoke about people who'd had cancer. Tiff was so troubled by this (because it was something that was very close to the bone and we were very raw) that she decided to go for a run instead and left the meeting. Then about five minutes later, David Carr interrupted his talk and looked at me and said, "You, you've got a broken heart, haven't you?" I did! I had a completely broken heart. I had no idea what was left in me; where I was going; what God was doing. But I thought, *That's a bit general. It could be anyone.* He then said, "You've got a problem with your family."

'Now, to me, that was the rawest part of me, the rawest nerve. I could not comprehend how God had let my family go through that time — through the horrific, dehumanising humiliation of all the treatment; the burden that had placed on Tiff; and the fact that my children were growing up with me in bed, in hospital, no energy, bald, ugly and not fulfilling my role as a father or a husband. I had been in tears, weekly, in Tim Mayfield's flat, pouring out my heart to him and my anger and frustration about what I felt God had done to my family. So when David Carr said 'family' that really hit the mark.

# Such a Confirmation

'He then said, "Come here. I want to pray for you." He began to pray in a tongue that sounded like Mandarin Chinese. He was very forceful but he stopped himself, I think, after a couple of moments, and said, "This has been going on for three years, hasn't it?" which was such a confirmation, because it was three years since I had first had cancer. He then continued to pray and, fortunately, Paul Perkin and David Larlee came up and joined me, which gave me a degree of comfort, having been dragged out in front of 3,000 people to be prayed for. I remember him very clearly interrupting his Mandarin Chinese tongue by saying, "It is finished!"

'It was a very traumatic evening but it was so obviously God speaking because the words that were spoken were so direct, so personal and so apt, that nobody but God could have known. It left me in absolutely no doubt whatsoever that whatever the consequences of what had happened were — and the consequences took some time, several months, to work out — I was utterly, utterly convinced that God knew exactly where I had been for the last nine months.

## Why He was Silent

'I still haven't worked out why He was silent.  But I have come to understand and to learn that that is something which God does as a way of proving people's spiritual strength and their relationship with Him — a time of testing.  It's well documented throughout history. St John of the Cross called it "the dark night of the soul".  He experienced it and, in fact, William Wilberforce experienced it in the months before his calling to abolish slavery in the late 1700s.  So I've got a perspective on it now, but not a complete one.  What I do have is an utter conviction that God never ever leaves, that God does know what we're doing and that God is there.

## Spiritual and Psychological Healing

'It was a miraculous, prophetic word.  Was it healing?  I don't know.  I've had scans for another 12 months now and the cancer's not there.  Was that the high dose chemotherapy and stem cell transplant that I'd had the Easter before New Wine?  Maybe.  Was it a healing from God on that night?  Maybe.  What I did receive was a spiritual and psychological healing.  It was a U-turn.  From that day forward, I began to pick myself up.  So did my family — Tiff in particular.  It's taken some time, but God's intervention on that day was miraculous and life-changing.'

Praise God, James is still free of cancer today!

Still on the subject of healing, God's intervention helped Julian Churcher out one night too as we see next:

# The Power of Tongues

What would your reaction be if you had a child ill with pain in the middle of the night? Julian has a little five-year-old girl who woke up crying one night, hot and sweaty. The poor little thing was feeling distressed by pain in her legs. Now picture this: there's bleary-eyed  Daddy woken up by Mummy bringing her in to their bedroom. His first thought? *Oh, just let me sleep!* On second thoughts he says, "Let's pray and ask Jesus to make you better", although to be honest this was more out of desperation than expectation.

So Julian prays in tongues for a minute.

Instantly his little girl calms down and perks up. Surprised, she asks, "Daddy, what did you do?"

"It wasn't Daddy but Jesus making you better," he explains. Then she remembered how Daddy had prayed once before like that and the pain had gone away. She certainly learned an important lesson about the power of praying in the Spirit that night!

The problem is, it's the middle of the night and she's become ridiculously bouncy and amused by the whole thing. Well, when the Healer touches you, what else would you expect?! Goodnight, sweetheart, Daddy needs his sleep now.

With that, it's lights out for this chapter too.

# 3. Adults at New Wine

145 people from St Mark's went down to New Wine in Shepton Mallet this year (2007) out of a total of 11,000 people. Here's a few of us sharing what God did during that very special week.

## A Slice of Heaven on Earth

Andy after his second time at New Wine answers: What did God do for you this time?

'So much, I feel compelled to share some of the joy we had and, despite the tents, despite the appalling downpour on Saturday night — and some of you may have been thinking, *I'm glad I'm not there!* — come next year. Please come and join us! I went last year ... and I was transformed. I learned how to understand what it means to give my sin to Jesus. So I went with great expectations this year. I had the suspicion in my mind that *God lives in Shepton Mallet*. And it's true! It's official! He does! What I learned this year was *why* God lives in Shepton Mallet...

'Half way through the week, there was a pastor, a wonderful, Pentecostal pastor, Pastor Agu. One of the texts he picked out was one early in Acts after Pentecost on the fellowship of the believers. How they have *apostolic teaching*; they have *fellowship*; they *break bread* and they devote themselves to *prayer*. And we know what happened to that church! God rained His blessings down — His Spirit came down and they transformed the Western world. I sat there and I listened to that and I thought, *That's why God's here, because this is what we're doing: we are living in the model of the apostolic church.* We had *teaching* that you couldn't believe. It was the most wonderful, inspired teaching; it was so stirring. We had *fellowship* in bucket loads. Old friendships were being strengthened; new friendships were being born. We were in and out of each other's tents. We were eating food together. There was such love in that place. We *broke bread*, not just in the sense that we shared food, but we broke bread in remembrance of Jesus. Everything was centred on Jesus: why we were there; why it was we were saved. And we *prayed.*

'Louise and I have struggled with prayer; struggled with being able to find the words at prayer time. But the Spirit of prayer in that place was awesome, absolutely awesome ... and the words came. Why did the words come? Because we were *living* in that apostolic tradition. And God is good. God is faithful. God does what He says He will do. He did it then. He will do it now. Pastor Agu said to us, "Take it back to your churches. Make connections with the churches around you." We *can* have revival. We saw it in that place. Someone said to me on the last night — and they weren't trying to be metaphorical — they said, "This is a slice of heaven on earth. It is a 'breaking through'." It was! *Please* come and join us next year!'

## Bondage Broken

Marianne Bolton wasn't at New Wine for the first time, though it was her first time in about 10 years. We asked her, 'What did God do in your life during the week at New Wine?'

'I think, actually, it wasn't until the very end of the week. I went to a seminar by Frog and Amy Orr-Ewing — fabulous names! [They are on the New Wine Leadership Team.] I wasn't going to go to the seminar, but it was raining so I thought, *why not?*

'Very briefly, Frog talked about how he was bullied at school. This is an experience which happened to me as well, and it had been affecting how I'd been relating to people in the group while I was there. I was having all the paranoia about: *Do people really like me? Do people really accept me?* It's been 20 years, but it's still a problem. I went to this talk; heard him share; saw just how God was working in his life. It was a real encouragement that you can go through these really horrendous things and you can either let it make you bitter or you can use it for God's glory. *He* was using it for God's glory. It felt like it broke a bondage in me. It was the second to last day, but from that moment onwards, I've felt so free. I felt like it was the first time that week I could really worship God — and it was amazing!'

## Have I Ever Told You God Loves You?

Angie was there for her fifth time.

'When I arrived, I was amazed because there were a lot of us. The teaching was wonderful and we all had a wonderful time within our villages. The whole emphasis over the week was mission from the churches and to go out into our community. And that we, in our local churches, are the only ones who can make a difference. What it culminated in for me was a speaker called John Coles who, on the last night, said, "I'm going to give you three words: *just do it!*" He continued, "I'm going to do something I've never done before. Who's got a mobile phone?" We all put up our hands. He said, "Right, now I want you all — and I know some of you are older and can't text so fast — but I want you all to text a friend to say, 'Have I ever told you that God loves you? I'll speak about this later.'"

'So we all got out our mobile phones. It was quite extraordinary, all four and a half thousand of us texting somebody that God loves them. Quite scary really! But the most amazing thing happened. It has opened up myriads of conversations for me since I got back. I think doing something for God and literally to *just do it* — not think about it, not think about it next week, to *just do it* — was fantastic and it really inspired me.'

## The Effect of the Holy Spirit

For Christine Fisher, it was her first time at New Wine. What did God do in that week for her?

'Well, um ... I was touched by the Holy Spirit for the first time in my life,' she says, almost in a whisper. [*Applause from the congregation.*]

'Awesome!' says David Larlee interviewing her, 'How were you prayed for?'

'It was in one of the evening sessions and they just told me to let go — let go and receive all His goodness. I was glued to the seat for ages but someone encouraged me to get up and walk to the front. And that was it; I couldn't walk home! My friend was staying right the other end in the pink [section]. We were in the blue [section] at the opposite end of the camp and I had to walk home on my own. I was wobbling all over the place! One of the daughters from this church was on her bike and she recognised me. She's only 13. She stopped and she cycled with me all the way back to our camp. I just thought that was really sweet of her.'

'Although it's only days since New Wine ended, what difference has that made? Now that you're back home, have you seen the difference?' 'I feel a lot happier.' [*More applause.*]

## The God of Chance Encounters

'Christine, is this your first time at New Wine?' [*Everyone laughs.*]

'Fifth time,' says Christine Perkin, 'and if *I* can camp, *anyone* can camp, although they all tell me I let them down dreadfully, because this year we were in a caravan! Yes, this whole week was about getting out there and taking Jesus out there. For me, there were many, many things; but one little thing to share was confirmation that God is the God of chance encounters.

# Confirmation

'It was after a main meeting. A woman came up to me and said, "You won't remember me from last year, but I'm the woman in the white skirt."

'I looked and said, "Sorry, I actually don't."

'She said, "Well, we were passing each other last year across the field and, as we were passing, you said, 'What a lovely white skirt.' Then you took another look and you saw that I was upset. So you said, 'Can I pray for you?' As you prayed, you quoted something out of Song of Songs: *Many waters cannot quench love; rivers cannot wash it away.* It was a very brief prayer and we then both moved on, but you hadn't realised that was about my tenth confirmation that I should go back to my husband. We'd been estranged for four years at that time. We got back together and it was as if nothing had gone wrong between us. We are so happy."

'Isn't that wonderful? He's the God of chance encounters.'

Yes, it certainly is wonderful — and so is our God!

# 4. Just Visiting

Have you ever been a visitor to St Mark's?  Or do you like to bring visitors?  John and Wendy Hall (standing on the left and the right in the picture), who normally prefer to come to the early nine o'clock service, brought a Dutch visitor on one occasion.  Nanette (centre) Bijkerk-Postma's life was changed forever by her visit to us.

## Asked to Help Out

John, a retired clergyman, had been asked to help out with a chaplaincy at a church in Heiloo, Holland, until a permanent chaplain could be found.  It was at this time that John and Wendy settled into a house,

bought by the church, opposite Nanette and her family.  Nanette had been very helpful during the redecoration of the house, so John and Wendy were told, 'If you need anything, or need to ask anything, go to Nanette.'  That's how they came into contact with her.

John says, 'She spoke very good English.  She was very kind and showed us how things worked, where they were, lent us what we needed, translated for us, dealt with the gas man and such like.  It worked out very well and we really made a friend of her.'

Nanette now continues with her side of the story:

# Why?

'At Easter the church had an Easter egg hunt. John and Wendy invited us to come but, as my husband, Peter, (pictured left) is not a Christian, I just went there with my son, Eric. We had a lovely time and got to know John better. My first question to John was, "Why is Easter always on a different day?" I'd asked this before but there was no one who could give me the answer. I also asked, "But why is Christmas always on the same day? Is that when Jesus was born?"

'He said, "No, no one knows when Jesus was born. They just picked a date." He gave me more answers and that's how our relationship started. I then started going along to the church in Heiloo. The people at the church became friends with Peter (who has been very supportive and now helps in the church) and we grew closer to John and Wendy.

# Special

'When I visited London one and a half years later with my family, John and Wendy asked if I would like to go to the service at St Mark's. The service was completely different from ours in Holland. We went to the 10.30 a.m. family service. The music was very lively with violin and so on. People were there talking about the experience of New Wine and that was so special. There was one person giving a testimony at the sharing spot who told how he had been in prison and about all the support he had been given from St Mark's when he came out. He was almost in tears.

'Another testimony was from a couple who'd had relationship problems and also problems in believing. They had gone to a session at New Wine, during which the men had gone upstairs and the women downstairs. In their [separate] meeting rooms this couple had fallen on their knees at the same time and had prayed out loud. That touched me! They had had the same experience because they had both felt the presence of God and, at that moment, He had worked in their hearts.  Since then their relationship has been good.

## Prayer

'The whole service was so special.  I'm a very emotional person yet, during the service, I felt a peace come over me.  I don't know what happened.  My heart had been touched.  After the service, we went outside to John and Wendy's car.  We were sitting in the car and John gave me three prayer points and said they could pray for me in the car.  That was completely new to me!  We prayed for my husband; we prayed for my son; then we prayed for my back because I had a hernia and a lot of back problems.  John put his hand on my back, on the spot where I had pain and his hand burned.  That's how it felt.  As he prayed, it became hotter and hotter.  A day later, I went home and my back pain was not so bad anymore.  There was still some pain there, but not how it had been before prayer.

## Decision to Live for God

'After this new experience I decided to go to the new chaplain and his wife in Heiloo, Roy and Joke [pronounced 'Yoka'] Ball, and start Bible studies.  I wanted to know more about God, how Christianity works and what it means to be a believer.  Then I decided to be baptised.  It was during the service at St Mark's that I had made my decision to live for God and subsequently during the prayer time in the car.  That's how it came together.

'Because of that moment at St Mark's and because I knew them, I asked John and Wendy to come to my baptism.  They arranged things so that they could come to my baptismal service.  John and the new chaplain, Roy, baptised me together.  That was very unusual because it isn't normally done by two people.  So that made it special.  Some of my family members who are not Christians came too, which I really appreciated.'

## The Power and Presence of God

At her baptism Nanette said, 'For much of my life I have been interested in faith in God.  But for so long, many of my questions remained unanswered.  Often I felt a kind of emptiness and unhappiness inside. When John and Wendy became our neighbours... they were normal people and very friendly. I was able to put my questions to them and finally got answers. Their talk about God was like taking the lid off a cookie box to see what was inside! When my family visited them in England, I went with them to a church service. During that service, I felt a great calm descend on me and I felt the power and presence of God. Since that day, I have known that God will always be there for me and that I can rely on Him.' That's faith!

## 'My Eyes Were Completely Healed!'

Nanette's faith has grown since then. She shares, 'For seven years I wore glasses and for two years I suffered from headaches, specifically above the eyes. I found reading difficult. The optician said he couldn't do anything so maybe I had some eye disease. My church in Heiloo prayed for me. Then I went to the hospital to check things out. They ran some tests and found out that there was nothing wrong with my eyes. My eyes were completely healed! Now I don't need to wear glasses anymore and I no longer suffer from the specific headaches that I used to get. I am so very grateful.'

What an encouragement to everyone's faith! God is so good.

# 5. Children's Work

For the children at New Wine, a new model of prayer ministry had been developed. It was to have a shack at the back, open for prayer for about three and a half hours in the morning, outside of the worship and the talk. The children would come for prayer for healing either for themselves or relatives; for people they wanted to pray for to become Christians; because they'd had a picture; because they felt God was speaking to them; or, indeed, for any other reason. Steve and Hayley were helping out in a team of five with Rock Solid, for the eight- and nine-year-olds. There were 600 of them and Steve starts with the story of the difference they made with one of those children.

## Virtually Inconsolable

'There's one particular kid who sticks in my mind. He was called James and he turned up on about the second evening. He was virtually inconsolable. He was *really* crying, bawling and petrified. There was a lot of loud music and dancing about, so I decided to take him outside where it was a bit quieter, to calm down a little. I've *never* seen a kid *so* distraught. He was *really, really* scared of the devil.

# 'If God Wants Me to Lay Down My Life...'

 'He'd been reading a lot of Revelation, obviously on his own, and had interpreted it in a 'Lord of the Rings' style for an eight-year-old. He'd got himself very frightened and worked up. So we prayed with him and he calmed down a bit, but we were still worried about him after that first evening. He turned up the next morning when he was a little bit calmer and had all these questions about the Bible. He'd obviously read huge chunks of the Bible and he was asking all sorts of complicated questions: questions that I only recently started asking like, "If God wants me to lay down my life and hate my mother and father and go out to be a missionary, then, you know, I'm only eight, how am I supposed to do that?" So I showed him parts of the Bible which said, "Don't worry," and told him that, "Unless you specifically heard from God that you should be a missionary now, I think that's fairly unlikely. And you can always check these things with your children's church leader or your mum and dad."

## Totally Confident in God

'We prayed for him and simply asked God to show him one little way, one little thing, that he could sacrifice for God's work, then told him he should go and check that with his parents and see how he gets on. "Just start small." Anyway, he came back that evening after they'd had the afternoon off. He'd been playing with some older boys and girls in his group and they'd been making these little things they call 'Scooby Doos' which are like little geometric patterns you can make out of plastic wire. They decided they were going to make these and sell them to make some money. They'd basically decided after making these — they'd got a bit convicted — that they were going to give the money to charity. Well, it turns out that by that time in the evening, they'd already made something like £53 for charity. They'd decided to give this money to a charity that had a display at New Wine which helped orphaned kids in other countries. This guy, James, was elated that he'd actually found — or God had given him — something to do that was just giving up a bit of his time and he was helping other people. From that point on, he really changed. We were praying about all sorts of things, when he became more relaxed, more confident. We couldn't get rid of him by the end of it! He was actually praying for other kids and helping them to get closer to God. He just wasn't worried any more or scared of the devil, but was totally confident in God and was praying for healing for other kids. That was *really* good to see!'

Now over to Hayley for more of what God did in the children's lives:

## Chocolate and the Book of Exodus

'We were invited to do a seminar on practical prayer and the team leader did one on the passion of prayer for us. The theme for the week was Exodus and the Israelites being freed from slavery in Egypt. So I decided to take up the theme of modern-day slavery with the children. We talked about children being slaves to produce cocoa because that's quite relevant to kids. We talked about what we felt prayer meant, what we felt slavery meant and how both of them were a bit of a surprise, because slavery is something that we think is in the past. We don't realise that sometimes we ask *Jesus* to change things and He tells *us* to go and make the change.

'So we shared with the children how they could go and make a difference by buying Fairtrade chocolate and how they could encourage their friends, the tuck shops, the supermarkets and their parents. We also invited them to draw or write postcards to the Prime Minister telling him what they felt about other children being used as slaves. And what God felt about it. They were really poignant postcards. There were going to be another 300 or 400 postcards coming from New Wine Central and New Wine South-West as well.' [Hayley's group was New Wine London.]

Here are some examples of what the children wrote:

'We need to make everyone eat Fairtrade chocolate to stop children about my age working day and night to make our chocolate. They are too young to work so hard. Even the adults are working too hard. Please help. It could change people's lives for ever.'

'I think slavery is horrible. Please will you stop it because some people, even children, are getting treated horribly?'

'Please help the slaves who have to make our chocolate. It isn't fair that we enjoy chocolate while they have to make it. God would not want it to be like this and neither do we.'

'Please stop! In Africa there are children in slavery. I will only eat Fairtrade chocolate until a new law is made.'

'I want you to do something about slaves in Africa. They are just as good as us.'

'Stop the unfair trade! P.S. Otherwise I won't like you.'

## Transformed into the Likeness of Christ

'Among lots of different healings and pictures that the children had, a little girl I prayed with wanted to pray for her sister. She said, "God has given me a picture."

'I said, "What's the picture of?"

'"It's my sister looking into a mirror and the reflection is God."

'In our team time, we'd been looking at Romans 8. Unwittingly, this eight-year-old had come up with being transformed into the likeness of Christ, probably, without even knowing that that was in the Bible. Quite amazing!

## A Huge Man... with Big Yellow Wings

'Another little boy I was praying with had been praying regularly for his family to become Christians: aunts, uncles and cousins on several evenings.    One evening we were praying and he said, "I've got a picture."

'"What's your picture?" I asked.

'"Well, you see the doors?" (We were sitting in a cattle shed.) "The door is pushed right back and there's a huge man standing in the door and he's got big yellow wings."

'So I turned round going, "Where is he?  Where is he?"  It was really exciting.

## Crutches Thrown Away on Stage!

'One particular little girl I prayed with was called Penny.  She came on the Monday and told me that her mum had had a really swollen knee for a couple of months.  She couldn't walk properly and this was obviously causing her quite a few problems.  I don't know if she worked, but she was trying to look after her family and couldn't get around.  So I prayed quite a silly prayer: that she would be able to skip and run and jump.

'On the Wednesday Penny came back and said, "Oh, I just want to let you know, my mum is really confident on her crutches." I thought, *Ooh that's exciting! God's done quite a lot of work.* Then on the Thursday she came back and said, "My mum's *running*!" I was thinking, *That's ridiculous!* The Prayer Shack team leader contacted her parents and asked if they'd be willing to give their testimony at the family celebration.  They were, and on the Friday afternoon her mum got up and threw her crutches away on the stage!  It was really exciting!

## Headaches Flushed Away!

'We had a spate of headache healings.  One little boy came to the Prayer Shack with a wet paper towel on his head to soothe his headache.  The Medical Square team were bringing the children to the Prayer Shack to be healed.  Steve prayed for him; he went away and wasn't feeling much better.  But then he went to the toilet and flushed the tissue away — and he was healed!  After that, we had two or three more children come with headaches. We told them to throw the tissue away — and they were healed too!

## Vision of a 'Shiny Man'

'Regarding pictures and visions, there was one girl who came and told me she'd had a recurring picture that God kept giving her. Generally, children, like adults, probably don't remember exactly from one day to the next how they described things. Yet, she had told exactly the same picture to another leader in the Prayer Shack the previous day. She came to me and said, "I had this picture and it's a mountain and I'm walking up the mountain…" — it's like a vision really — "and there's always somewhere to sleep and there's always somewhere to eat and I keep walking. When I get to the top of the mountain there's a gate and there's a garden. And there's a beautiful crystal lake and there's a shiny man…" She said, "But this time, today, Jesus is walking up the mountain with me and He's stopping with me and eating with me. Then, when we get to the top, He goes to speak to the 'shiny man'" (or goes to stand next to him, I can't remember which). It was quite interesting!

## Dream Interpretation

'A little boy had dreamt in his sleep and had seen a person, a number three, an arrow and some gates. He came back to Steve and he said, "Right, I've got this picture and I want to know what it all means — and God's already told me what the arrow and the gates mean."

'Steve said, "Okay, what did God say?"

'"The arrow means *follow* and the gates mean *heaven*." Steve started explaining how we need to weigh up whether things are from God or not.

'The little boy said, "Oh, yes, I've already done that! I've received some other pictures and I know they weren't from God."

'Steve asked, "What were they then?"

'"A crocodile and a fire exit." So they prayed about the person and the number three. The boy felt that God was saying the person was a *person* and the number three was *God*, so *follow God to get to heaven* was the interpretation of the dream he'd had.

'Children just expect things to happen straight away, so quite a lot of the time they'd get prayed for and say, "Oh that feels better now." They've got no reason to believe anything should be difficult and they find it much easier to hear from God. If you tell children to listen to God, they just go, "Oh okay, I'll listen to God," and they write it down — or whatever you ask them to do.'

Children have a simple faith, don't they?

# 6. Soul Survivor

Soul Survivor 2007 (a Christian camping conference for teens) took place straight after New Wine down in Shepton Mallet. Gareth Wallace tells us what his experience of the event was like:

## Passionate

'My little brother and I went — 'little' meaning he's 20 and I'm 27 — so I felt a bit old, but I was hanging out with a friend of mine who's a youth worker at St Margaret's in Uxbridge and her group of teenagers. It was horribly wet and windy — tents were blowing away and rain was pouring down — thoroughly miserable weather, but the actual festival itself was amazing, fantastic. They had more  people at Soul Survivor than at any other previous year and Week B [18th to 22nd August] was the busiest.

'With all the Soul Survivor weeks put together there were 28,000 people! [Add to that all the New Wine people, there was something like 50,000 people down at Shepton Mallet!] At this Week B event there were 12,000 young people. There was lots of life, lots of vibrancy and lots of stuff going on. But I suppose the most interesting thing was just seeing how *passionate* they all were.

# My Knee Healed!

'One night we were praying for healing and some of the teenagers from St Margaret's prayed for my knee. It was happening all around the massive marquee. There was no special prayer ministry doing this; it was just the teenagers themselves praying for each other. I'd had a twinge in my knee from cycling my bike and I was going climbing in the Alps with a group of friends. I thought, *I just want to be better! I should be buying creams and those stretchy sock things. What a load of nonsense!* Yes,  I can get those things but when the opportunity is here — in fact the opportunity's always there but especially now — it would be good to get it prayed for. They prayed for me and I didn't feel anything particularly special, and I thought, *Oh well, maybe not this time.* My brother also prayed for my knee.

## 'It's Been Completely Different Since'

'As the prayer ministry time wore on, people were coming up with amazing testimonies. Dozens of people were declaring healings of knees, arms, heads, hands and backs. A couple of hours after prayer, whenever I moved it, I could feel the twinge in my knee was going and it's been completely different since. Certainly before prayer, whenever I was driving the car, if I'd been cycling for a while, or if I'd been sitting for a long time and then got up, I would definitely feel it again. For a couple of weeks it just didn't seem to want to go away. I'd be thinking, *I'll have to take this to the doctor.* But now it seems fine, so I've no excuses with my friends while climbing.'

Since his holiday, we got in touch with Gareth to check how the knee was. His answer: 'I suffered many more aches and pains while climbing; it was much more demanding than I expected. But *the knee was great!*' Hey, isn't that good? Praise God for the healing!

# Endless Worship

Gareth continues, 'The worship was led by a 20-year-old and there was a 20-year-old speaker, who spoke with *no notes* in front of a crowd of thousands of teenagers. The leaders were incredibly gifted people who were all so humble with their giftings. It was really inspiring to watch. Mike Pilavachi [the founder and leader of Soul Survivor] was a brilliant, really good, relevant, well-thought through, evangelical speaker. He made sure that he demystified everything about the Holy Spirit ministry that was going on. It was such a big venue; Mike was speaking and explaining what was happening, especially when people were crying out either in pain or laughter. This happened every night depending on what people were being prayed for.

'He was saying, "Don't be alarmed by this. Don't be freaked out by that. It's just the way the Spirit's working in people. They might have deep hurt in them that they haven't really been able to express before and *that's* being healed."

'The times of ministry would go on longer than the talk or the worship times, maybe an hour, or an hour and a half, and after that they'd *still* want to stay around and sing. Then there was the 'after hours' worship which was always packed out full of teenagers singing their hearts out. Yeah, it was a *really* inspiring time!'

Samuel Verbi, who was one of our youth worship leaders until recently, gives his take on the Soul Survivor experience:

# Absolutely Wild for Jesus

'16- to 17-year-olds are always very self-conscious about what their friends are thinking. Yet I found it was the complete opposite in this situation. They were jumping up and down, waving their hands in the air... [and generally being very expressive] which really helped *me* to worship God because everyone was putting in that much effort. It was such an *amazing* experience to be right at the front and to have over 10,000 self-conscious teenagers behind me going absolutely wild for Jesus. We had to make sure we were there an *hour* before the main session started to get seats at the front. As soon as the doors opened we had to run.'

Wow! It does sound like the worship was fantastic, doesn't it?

# 7. Prison Alpha and Beyond

## Saved Through Prison Alpha

Jamie Lincoln has now joined the church plant to St Peter's Church, Battersea. We first met him through Prison Alpha. This is how he came to Christ in Wandsworth Prison. He wrote his testimony in poetic form:

> I look out my prison cell window
> And I watch the world go by.
> I think of life and I start to cry,
> Isolated from a world I once lived but I failed.
>
> At night I would roam the streets,
> To find some sort of peace
> But I just ended up on stairs,
> Smoking crack to escape a world that doesn't care.
>
> Fifteen years old,
> No-one to hold,
> Just a young boy,
> Flowing in the wrong river.

The prison walls are so silent
It makes me remember my life of violence.
A young misunderstood,
Freedom is what I tried to find but I never could.

At the age of twenty I sat in a prison cell
And looked at my life,
And remembered how I fell,
A broken heart tired of life's disgrace.

So I got on my knees and confessed
I was a sinner and God saved me with his grace.
In my dreams I'm breaking free from this misery.
Jesus is the light in the darkness.

## Prayers for Healing Answered

Najeeb came up to the microphone to say, 'Just a quick thank you to the Lord. A lot of you don't know this but my mum was taken into hospital. It came as quite a shock as it came completely unexpectedly. We've been praying. She's on the road to recovery. She had to go in overnight. Apparently they didn't drain all the fluid on her lungs but they got most of it. She's on the way to recovery, so praise God for healing'.

We've since caught up with Najeeb to check how his mother is. He shared how, 'her healing approximately eight years ago led me to finally see the Lord's grace and love. God has blessed my family with eight more years with my mother. Although the cancer (lymphoma) has come back in a more serious form, He is faithful and through the power of prayer, the Lord can bless us with more years with my mother if that's His plan. Let the Lord's will be done for He is good, kind and loving.'

# 'Najeeb, How Did You Become a Christian?'

That was the unexpected question Paul Perkin asked Najeeb, when he came up to the microphone with the testimony of his mum's healing.

*Najeeb*: 'Alpha.'

*Paul*: 'And out of what kind of religious background?'

*Najeeb*: 'An interesting one! I'm of mixed parentage. My father was from Pakistan, so there's Muslim from my father's side of the family. My mum is Irish/Welsh mix, so there's Catholicism, sort of, in the mix there as well.'

*Paul*: 'And what happened to you on Alpha out of this Catholic/Muslim background?'

*Najeeb*: 'Well, even though I had that parentage and that heritage in my family, I wasn't raised up in a religious way at all. But back before I became a Christian, I was going through quite a difficult time and also, again, my mum was sick and I needed some support. I basically came to St Mark's. I was living with a long-standing member of St Mark's, Ross Tulloch. I was one of his many lodgers. Also a friend was living there. I was encouraged to come to St Mark's which, eventually, I did after lots of umming and ahing and saying no. Eventually I thought, *Well, I've got nowhere else to go — I've got to give it a try.*'

*Paul*: 'And you found Jesus on the Alpha Course?'

*Najeeb*: 'I did.'

*Paul*: 'How many years ago?' [*Pause*] 'About five years ago?' [*Pause*] 'More?'

*Najeeb*: 'More ... more! Nearly nine years now, wow!'

# 8. Coping with Death

Ed and Cara Verbi shared with us, their church family, so bravely, after the death of Cara's dear sister (in November 2007).

## 'We Want to Say Thank You'

Ed began simply by saying, 'Thank you very, very much for standing with us as we shared on two occasions about Cara's sister, Vicky, who six months ago was diagnosed with liver cancer. We stood here on those occasions categorically stating that we knew and firmly believed that God was going to heal her. Well, she died three weeks ago. But, nevertheless, we want to say thank you.'

Cara then shared, 'I wanted to actually do this without notes but I don't think I'm going to hold it together, so in fact what I'm going to do is read out an email which some of you may have read. Ed and I were emailing a group of people every week with news of Vicky, really, for the last six months and some of you were on that email list so these words won't be new to you. Whether you were on the list or not, I know that many of you were aware of what was going on and, led by Paul, prayed for Vicky and Chris, the family and all of us over the months. So thank you very, very much indeed for that.

## Utterly Precious

'This is the email: The past six months have been a journey, believing, looking out for and pressing in to the wholeness which we believe God wants for us here on earth. From the moment in April when Vicky and I boarded a plane to visit Bill Johnson's church [in Redding, California] for a long weekend, it has been a mission step by step with darling Vicky. It was the greatest privilege to walk so closely alongside her and to keep pressing in to the God, whom Vicky knew was her Healer. She held on until the end. The part you all played in this journey has been utterly precious and we could not have done it without you. To know that you were with us as a family in prayer and fasting means more to us than we can ever say.

## Something Dynamic, Explosive and Fruitful

'Amidst all the pain and heartbreak — everything's still so raw — I am so profoundly sure that God heard every single prayer; and that, in those unseen heavenly places, there is even now a rumbling and a shifting as territory, which was illegally taken by the enemy, is being regained. We are in a fierce battle! We all walk this together and I feel certain that this is not the end but actually the continuation of something dynamic, explosive and fruitful. For my part, amidst all the tears and grief at the loss of a precious sister, I'm determined that we should keep moving, so that what, six months ago, seemed immovable should, in the future, be seen to be really, really possible. I know that Vicks would be, and probably is, urging us to press in for more of the reality of His kingdom here on earth.

## Angels' Feathers

'Stephen [Ruttle], our brother, and I had a little understanding with Vicky about angels' feathers and would often retrieve little white feathers and give them to her saying, "Look Vicks, angels' feathers!" This, in fact, we did just a day or so before she died. She was in a hospice and we found a little fluffy pigeon feather. We took it in to her and said, "Look Vicks, angels' feathers." This was said with a chuckle, but each one of us really hoped that one day God would surprise us with the real thing! Very movingly, Stephen placed two little feathers on her pillow on that last morning: a symbol of the nearness of the kingdom of God and of our quest together to see more of His kingdom and wholeness on earth.

## 'I Never Want to Go Back to Normal!'

'So thank you for your commitment and for loving and fighting for our Vicky. What a joy to know that one day we will be together forever in heaven. I can't wait! But there is still more to do here. And the 'more' for me in a nutshell is this: that I don't ever want to go back to normal again. Six months ago I was in 'normal'; it was quite comfy and I've had to get out of that boat during the last six months. And I never want to go back to normal! So I'm asking

Vicky

you as my family to make sure, if you see me being normal say, "Come on Cara! What's going on? Press on!" I want to press on. I want to take risks. I want to get out of the boat and I want to go for that raw power of God which Vicky, only two days before she died, when she could hardly actually talk and a team from California were praying with her, was just saying, "the raw power of God, the raw power of God." That's what I want.'

## 'Hold On to What We've Learned'

Ed continues, 'It was a double blow for us, because we categorically and firmly believed that it was God's will to heal Vicky; not only that it was God's will, but that it was going to happen. So we've had a double loss, if you like. We've lost darling Vicky. And our faith? We have lots of questions, but we've taken great encouragement from what Bill Johnson has said. And for all of us here, there have been many occasions, I'm sure, when we've prayed — when we've felt that God has spoken — and it doesn't happen. Now, in those situations, there can be bitter disappointment. Bill Johnson lost his father through cancer; he lost his secretary through cancer. This is what he says, "The one thing that we must do in disappointment is to hold on to what we've learned. The one thing you do not want to do is to devalue what God has taught you." He says, "I don't understand everything, but I *must* hang on to what I do understand — in disappointment."

'What happens is that we start sacrificing what God's given us, all that we've learned and all that we've received from God in the last few months. It would now be so easy to sacrifice that, to make sense of the disappointment and to devalue all that He's given us. No! Don't! We don't understand what's happened, but hold on; hold on to what we've learned! Bill went on to say, "I've piles of questions that I don't understand, but if I allow those things to take away from what I *do* understand — and that's the power of disappointment — then I'm trading truth for a lie." So hold on! We've all been there. We *will* go there I've no doubt. We must press on for more of His kingdom here on earth. Thank you, guys, *so* much.'

# 9. Growing Through Alpha

There's an international flavour to our Alpha testimonies this time. Meet two people born the same distance from London but in opposite continents, who both grew in faith through our very own Alpha Course. First up Luke Raskino from Bombay (now Mumbai):

## Christianity... Rather Embarrassing

'My dad came home one day and said, "I want to be a better man." He went on a retreat, came back and had become a Christian — at which point he changed rather dramatically! I was going to a public school in India and my dad, very soon after, quit his job, began talking about Jesus to people in the street and basically started being very embarrassing. He'd go to school on his scooter with 'Jesus loves you' written on it. I would effectively run for the hills! So my first interactions with Christianity were rather embarrassing. Funnily enough, my first commitment to Jesus was also fairly embarrassing, because I got myself hopelessly drunk at a party, came home at four o'clock in the morning and thought I was going to get a right rollicking! To avoid the onslaught, I told my dad that I'd become a Christian. The guy got so excited, he actually got me baptised the following day! But it was only about six months after that he realised what was driving it, i.e. that in effect I had faked my commitment.

## A Philosophical Journey

'Then I embarked on a philosophical journey. All the time, my father and I would have heated debates about Christianity. I would always find a couple of intellectual flaws in them, lose the debate and that was that. I'd walk away very frustrated. We did that for a few years and then I decided I needed to find answers for myself. So I went on a multi-religious, epic journey, trying to find out the truth. I landed up reaching quite an impasse philosophically, very influenced by Hinduism, in fact, where I suddenly started realising: *Who am I? People who know me; each one knows a different me. I think I know my mother but my dad knows a different mother and everybody else knows a different mother, so who are we? Nothing is real; everything is figments of imagination.* I was quite lost for some time.

## Message of Love

'Years passed and my wife, Sarah, and I moved to the UK. Sarah kept asking me, "Luke, will you come with me to church? Luke, come with me to church?" It was quite painful.

'Eventually I thought I'd get her off my back by saying, "Okay I'll go on an Alpha Course and if I'm not convinced at the end, never ask me ever again about religion. Don't give me any more hassle about church!"

'So she thought about it for a while and came back and said, "Okay". I thought to myself, *This is an incredible deal! It's win-win, my way!* So I did the Alpha Course.

'The first few weeks I was probably a huge pain in the proverbial, always asking the awkward questions. What really got to me was the message of love, that the one thing we have in common in this world is the fact that everybody wants to be loved. When I look at the message of Christ authoring the message of selfless love, at worst, it could be incredible for this world and at best, it's totally revolutionary. That really struck me! I thought to myself, *I've got sufficient here to embark on a journey.* I knew enough about Christ to want to embark on that journey. Since then, that's exactly what it's been. I've still got huge questions. Some of them have been so excitingly answered in the most phenomenal ways; others I'm still pressing on, debating. But it was on the Alpha Course, when Stephen Ruttle was leading it, that I actually became a Christian.'

Frank Madone originates from Littleton, Colorado in the beautiful Rocky Mountains of the USA. With his lovely, easy-listening American accent, he told us his story of how the Lord met him through the Alpha Course at St Mark's.

## Navy Days and Unholy Ways

'I was in the US Navy from 2000 to 2004 and sailors get up to stuff … so I got into a lot of trouble! I got into a lot of fist fights and almost got kicked out [of the navy]. I remember I was going down on watch and this guy was reading the Bible – it was the only book you could read when you were on watch – and I asked, "Why are you reading that?"

'Because we used to sneak books down he said, "Well, I'm going to read this first because this is truth." He was a really deep Christian! I sort of believed in it and thought, *Oh okay*.

'Then I got into trouble that week, while we were in Greece. I remember coming back to the ship and being told I was going to get kicked out and thinking, *God, please, please don't let me get kicked out*. I didn't really believe that God would answer my prayer. I went to jail (navy jail) for 45 days. I wrote a letter to the officer while in jail, explaining what had happened. The chaplain on the ship visited me and asked if I was religious, since I was wearing a cross, but I told him the cross was something my grandmother had given me. He prayed anyway. When I'd served my time, the captain said I wasn't going to get kicked out after all. This had *never* happened before! All of a sudden my prayer was answered and things turned!

# A Lot of Anger

'A year and a half later, when I got out of the navy, I moved here to London and started coming to church a bit, but didn't really believe in it. Then, because I had a lot of anger, a friend said to me, "Maybe you should come along to Alpha, if you've got loads of questions." I did the course once and people liked me and I thought, *Oh yeah I'm holy,* and I was asked back to be a helper. I was like the Christian who does something here in church, then goes away and does another thing; somebody who talked the talk rather than walked the walk.

## 'I'm Here to Do His Will'

'So I came back as a helper and went on the weekend away. I hadn't gone the first time. It was like a punch in the face; it was the biggest thing I'd ever experienced. Christ hit me! Andi Britt was leading a prayer, saying "If anyone feels a presence come over you, ask God to take control of you." I decided to try. A shock went through my body. I started speaking in tongues, even though I'd never heard tongues before! I just remember opening my eyes and feeling so different and thinking, *This is it — there's no going back!*

'Little things in my life started to change. I was still a bit angry. I met Clive [our former youth pastor] who took me under his wing and started asking me questions. Little by little and by the Holy Spirit, I started to change. There were little changes at first, like I quit biting my finger nails. Then I quit swearing. That one was hard! It took a while. But you start to change; your body starts to change and your mind and the way you think. And then I quit getting into fights. I used to get into loads of fights. I quit that and my anger subsided. I quit drinking. I don't drink now. Everything in my life has changed and you guys said to start reading the Bible, so I started reading the Bible a little bit. You find you get a sense of community, a sense of understanding about what God wants for you and wants for your life. I'm here to do His will, whereas before I was here to do my own will. And that's a huge change!'

Frank has been working with the youth for over two years now and says, 'I am so thankful for *inhabit*, the youth church. They've shown me just as much as I hope to have shown them.'

# 10. Christmas Hamper

Every December we make up Christmas hampers at St Mark's and then we give them to people in the community. Have you ever wondered how this might affect a person on the receiving end of such generosity? Debra Evans tells us her story:

## A Life of Drugs and Drink

'I was brought up as a Christian but my mum's Jewish and so the actual teaching that I learned was more Old Testament than New Testament. I was brought up to believe that God was a vengeful, angry God. I only asked for protection for family and loved ones — that kind of thing. But I was taught not to ask for anything specific like a new bike, for example. Then something happened to me when I was about eleven and I thought God was punishing me. I felt, *God, if you really loved me, you wouldn't let me go through what I'm going through.* I turned my back on God for twenty-odd years. I totally rebelled and lived a life of drugs (amphetamines) and drink. I had three relationships but never married and I had eight children.

'During those years three priests visited me. One was Catholic. He knocked on the door and said, "Can I bless this family?"

'"Go away!" I said politely. I moved again (I moved quite a lot) and it was a Church of England vicar this time, who knocked on the door to welcome me into the parish. Again I said, "Go away!" The third time, the same thing, "Leave me alone!" I still blamed God for everything.

## Wandsworth Prison

'My life got very, very chaotic. My second partner, a lapsed Roman Catholic, died from illness. I always believed that there was something, but I was just so angry with God. He was easy to blame for everything that was going wrong and I was in the grip of my addiction.

'My last partner, who I've split up with now, went to Wandsworth Prison. He got three and a half years and met Tim Mayfield on the Alpha team. In prison he did the Alpha Course, and the RAPt [Rehabilitation for Addicted Prisoners trust] course, as well. He mentioned St Mark's to me, saying, "Why don't you go to St Mark's?" When he came out on home leave, we came to St Mark's but, because I had such a low opinion of myself and saw all those happy, smiley faces, I thought, *Oh You wouldn't like me if You knew what I've been up to.* So I kept everyone at a distance.

## The Real Turning Point

'The real turning point was when Tim Mayfield and Sarah Spreckley came round with a Christmas hamper. I'll never forget it as long as I live! I was still using drugs and drinking. They turned up and I had six boys living at home then. I had a flood and the house was chaotic; the kids were running around. There were these two happy, smiley people at my door with a big hamper and an envelope with a card in it. I just thought, *Wow, they look so happy!* I suppose it restored my faith in humanity because I didn't really have a lot of faith in people, let alone any other kind of faith.

# God Came into the Equation

'One night I was really, really out of my head, using [drugs]. I don't know if it was a spiritual awakening or God trying to get through to me, but I saw something fly past and actually felt it sit on my shoulder. I walked indoors and I just went to my son and said, "I'm not using no more!" I threw whatever drugs I had left down the toilet, went into my room and just fell to the floor and said, "Look, whatever You are, I just need help!"

'Then I went for my detox at home. Again, I started dipping into St Mark's and thinking, *Oh I don't know; I don't know*. Whenever I was in pain I kept coming to St Mark's and Sarah and Tim would pray for me outside. They'd sit there and pray and I'd be crying and sobbing. Little did I know at the time that God was working. I was just so relieved that I had somebody I could share all my pain with. And they'd always be there. And they'd always listen. Sarah would give me a mug of tea and we'd talk. And God came into the equation.

# A Lot of Shame

'I never really had a problem talking about God. It was Jesus that I struggled with because of the way I'd been brought up. I didn't understand that I could have a relationship with God through Jesus. Tim suggested I did the Alpha Course, so I went for about four weeks but thought, *No, I'm not getting this at all*. Again, I think that was down to low self-worth and low self-esteem. I didn't want people to know where I'd come from or what I'd done; I felt a lot of shame. Then I went into treatment and Tim visited me when I was in treatment. He had bought me a Bible. I used to read my Bible and *Daily Light* and do a gratitude list. When I first started with the gratitude list it had about two things on it. But by the time I finished, I'd be grateful for so many things.

# Struggling with the 'Jesus Bit'

'I moved house and made the decision to come to St Mark's every Sunday. Tim talked about doing the Alpha Course again, so I thought,

*Okay Debra, obviously something's happening but you're not sure what.* I did the Alpha Course and I was really honest and admitted to struggling with the 'Jesus bit'. I knew He was a man and He was very wise, but to believe that He's the Son of God when I was quite frightened of God...

'One day, there was something I specifically wanted. Tim said, "Debra you can pray for that."

'I said, "No, I can't." I had no problem praying to get well if I was ill, but not for a new house. I thought that if everybody asked for those things, God would be all over them; it just wasn't something you did!

'But Tim said, "No Debra, you *can* pray." So my prayers started changing.

## 'I Felt the Holy Spirit'

'When I did the Holy Spirit weekend, that just blew me away. *I felt the Holy Spirit!* That was really awesome! I was crying and had a big lump in my throat like a cat fur ball. I can remember being prayed for. I was physically sick and then my chest just expanded. I can remember saying to Tim, "What am I supposed to do now? My heart feels like it's just opened. I feel like I'm radiating this warmth and this love. Where do I put it?" I wasn't quite sure what to do with this feeling that I had. Now I know it was the Holy Spirit, but at the time I was walking around with a big grin on my face. That was really when I came to believe.'

Well, needless to say, there's a lot more of Debra's story, but praise God she finally joined the happy, smiley faces around St Mark's and now knows God as a loving Heavenly Father!

# 11. Alpha Course

The main Alpha Course runs in the autumn of each year. If you've been thinking of inviting someone, but haven't quite decided, maybe these testimonies will help you. Penny and Raj Parker have a combined testimony. They did Alpha a long time ago and they're *still* here, it made such an impact! First, Penny tells her side of the story:

## 'Why Don't *You* Go Along?'

'We did Alpha a long time back, but we were talking about it just the other day and it made us realise how fundamental it was to the fact that we *are* still here today some years down the line. Just a bit of background: I was brought up in a church-going family, but once I left home I became less committed and less involved. Then I met Raj — we met through work — and we got married. Raj's background is not Christian, but we were searching for something and we started going to Church in the City — one of those ones where they have a beautiful choir.

'We were always deeply affected by going, but we never quite found a home or a real understanding. We moved not far from St Mark's and decided that we would come and try out the local church on Sunday. We walked in and, given that my background was a fairly traditional Church of England church, I took one look at the screens and the guitars, practically turned on my heels and left! But Raj, who is clearly a far more open and understanding person than I am, was really intrigued so we stayed. Not long after we'd arrived, they started advertising the Alpha Course and, in my terribly stilted way, I said to Raj, "Well, this would be brilliant for *you* because I know all this stuff as I've done this for years; this is *perfect* for you. Why don't *you* go along to this course as it sounds really good?" So, off he went and did the course.'

## 'I Haven't Been the Same Since'

[At this point there is some hilarity while Penny hands over to Raj, rather than telling his story for him.] Diplomatically he says, 'Yeah, I agree with all that.' [*More laughter.*] Then Raj continues, 'Just three things to say: First of all, God was working because the house we bought was in the road that Paul and Christine [Perkin] live on — so we didn't really have much chance once that was done. Secondly, this Alpha Course is a fantastic thing in order for Christ to actually come into your life and change you. That's what He did for me 15 years ago and I haven't been the same since. The last thing to say is: Please, please, please invite people to it because it really isn't 'cringey' and it isn't threatening. Tim and his team do a fantastic job of making it really brilliant.'

## 'My Heart Had Changed'

Tim remembers Raj having said something significant after doing the Holy Spirit weekend and prompts him with, 'I remember you saying what it was like going into work the next day.'

Raj responds, 'Yes, when you get 'zapped' — some of you will know what that feels like, and others will find out — your whole outlook on people changes. I had been walking the same way to Clapham Junction for a few years and seeing the same faces; sometimes you look away or sometimes you look at people in a way that doesn't really do you much credit. That Monday morning after the Holy Spirit weekend, I started looking at people and wondering about their lives and looking at them as *people* for the first time. And that was a really practical demonstration that my heart had changed.'

## The Difference

'Penny, having Jesus in *your* life: What has the difference been for you?' asks Tim.

Penny answers, 'I think that the difference is having a new heart, really. A new heart changes how you go about your life and I guess over the process of time, my life has changed radically. God has moved me into completely different areas. Before I did the Alpha Course, if you had told me what I'd be doing now, I would never ever have believed you in a million years. For example, lots of work in prison: that was definitely a place where, if you'd told me even ten years ago that that's where I'd be working and really loving being, I would never have believed it. That is just a million miles from where I saw myself going, so I think it's incredibly exciting to have Jesus in your life and have potentially something really radical and different opened up in front of you.'

## Space and Time to Find God Again

Another person for whom the Alpha Course made a significant difference is Annie Sexton. Here is David Larlee's interview with her:

*David*: 'Annie, have you always been a Christian?'

*Annie*: 'I was a Christian as a teenager and then, after a huge hurt and disappointment, I wandered off and thought I could do it on my own.'

*David*: 'What made you do the Alpha Course?'

*Annie*: 'A friend of mine, who'd been a good friend for a long time, actually a member of the church here. We were talking one evening.

I was saying how disenchanted I was with life in general and she said, "You must do this course! It's a brilliant course." So she sent me the details.'

*David:* 'How did you find the course?'

*Annie:* 'Well, I was a little reluctant to start with. I think that I had a lot of barriers up which I wasn't prepared to drop. But the Alpha Course somehow gave me the space and the time to work through those issues that I had and it was extraordinary. It was an amazing journey. It was a very personal thing and I was given the space and the time to find God again.'

*David:* 'Tell us; what practical difference has Jesus made in your life?'

*Annie:* 'To start with, a lot of coincidences now happen in my life! Somehow, when I'm close to God, everything seems to mesh together and everything seems to make a lot more sense. I'm completely bowled over by an extraordinary amount of love that Jesus shows me. And that love is healing; it's guiding — and very 'happy-making' despite my unworthiness!'

These testimonies are surely an inspiration to do the Alpha Course if you've never experienced it — and bring your friends too!

# 12. Healing through Prayer

This is a heart-warming healing story of someone from the other side of the world, in which distance was no obstacle to the Lord. But then it never is. It's the testimony of Jane Campion and her father, Cecil, who lives in New Zealand.

## Diagnosed with an Incurable Disease

'In 2004, my father was diagnosed with an incurable progressive disease called Membranous Glomerulo Nephritis which affected his kidney function. It's very hard to diagnose the cause, but international rugby followers will remember the once-mighty Jonah Lomu and his battle with  kidney failure. My beloved stepmother then died of cancer with very little warning. Dad hardly had any time to mourn as he embarked on a course of chemotherapy and steroids, whose effects were nearly worse than the disease itself.

## Healing Service at St Mark's

'In Dad's words, "I've always known the Lord was there, but I was quite happy running my own life." I told him I was praying for him and would take him, by proxy, along to our Healing Service at St Mark's. He welcomed that and so I did take him, several times, with the team praying for him and anointing *me* with oil instead.

## 'Jesus Gave Me a Picture'

'Praying one day, Jesus gave me a picture of my father asleep in his bedroom which was suddenly filled with white light so intense that it filled my father as well. I came to understand, somehow, that this meant Jesus would save my father and that physical healing would also follow, so I kept praying this in, believing it would happen. In fact, I emailed a great many people around the world, asking for them to support my husband, Ross, and me in prayer.

'In 2005, Dad visited London and came along once to St Mark's with us. He was using a walking stick and his on-going health was a big concern. We talked a lot about Jesus during that visit and I told him about Alpha. I had already researched churches in his home town which ran courses. He seemed to take it in, but said little.

## The Miracle Began

'On his return home, the miracle began. He reported to me that the first Sunday he was home, he "heard someone say, 'put a tie on Cecil. You're going to church'." So he did. He drove out in the direction of his childhood home, "knowing I would know where to go when I got there", until he found a little Anglican church, St Oswald's. He began to go every Sunday and signed up for an Alpha Course!

## Saved and Born Again!

'Weeks later, I received an email which told me he had been on the Alpha weekend. It was just a scripture reference. I was in tears! I looked it up: *James and John laid hands on them and they received the Holy Spirit*. Dad was telling me that he had received the Holy Spirit! He was saved and born again! He went on to host a home group led by the vicar and his wife — parents of my childhood friend. This summer, Dad came to St Mark's once more. He was walking well unaided and his doctor took him off much of his medication in November 2007.

'He is now a keen and active member of his Christian family and spends time 'working for the Lord'. My Dad has new life and he has it abundantly. I am so grateful to everyone who prayed and to our Good Shepherd for going out to find a crusty old sheep lost out in the New Zealand hill country.'

Another New Zealander, Jo Mead, tells us about a very nasty accident that she had:

## Crushed Finger

'I was on my way to Italy on holiday with my daughter, Caley, who was three and a half years old at the time. I got out of the taxi cab and the taxi driver put the push-chair together. I glanced at it and thought it was fine. I put my daughter in it and a few seconds later it collapsed on her. The taxi driver, a passer-by and I all lunged at it. I grabbed the closest point that I could reach at the same time that the lady and the taxi driver put the push-chair back up and clicked it into place. It crushed my finger *completely*! My daughter was screaming; I was in agony!

'It took them a while to uncollapse the push-chair and get my finger out. When they did, it was almost completely flat and crushed. I remember feeling angry and thinking, *Lord I really want this holiday; I haven't had one in a long time.* I determined in my heart that I would go to the airport and get medical advice there. So I gathered my things with difficulty and got into the lift. A man next to me said, "You need to go to the hospital."

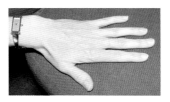

'At the same time Caley turned round and she said, "Don't worry, Mama. Jesus is going to heal your finger soon." I just can't tell you how flat my finger was!

'Over the next four hours it was as though my finger re-inflated. I gradually got the movement back. I didn't *even* have a black fingernail. I know that it was the faith of a child — uninhibited, uncluttered, pure faith.'

# 13. Home and Away

One of our prayer warriors, Elisabeth Nelson-Williams, has been away from her UK home and back to her original home, making a big difference. She will explain why:

## Away for Six Months

'I've been away for six months [October 2007]. I did not intend to be away for six months; I only went for three weeks. [But] my passport was stolen! I was going through immigration, got through and opened my case and I couldn't find my passport. There was some reluctance in issuing me a new passport until the Commonwealth Office ordered the British High Commission to provide me with one.

## Praying for 27 Years

My reason for staying [beyond that] — and that's what I want to give glory about — is that we had an election. My country of ethnicity is Sierra Leone. We've had a lot of problems. We've had a lot of war, but God has been faithful. We've had a government for ten years since the war, which has found it difficult to let go of power. But I stayed there because... I've been praying [for my country] for 27 years, ever since God woke me up and told me to take up my national anthem, which goes like this:

High we exalt thee, realm of the free;

Great is the love we have for thee;

Firmly united ever we stand,

Singing thy praise, O native land!

We lift up our hearts and our voices on high,

The hills and our valleys re-echo our cry

Blessing and peace be ever thine own,

Land that we love, our Sierra Leone.

## 'We Were in Slavery'

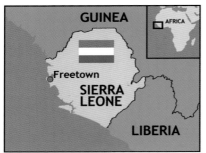

'But that is not what is happening in Sierra Leone at present and the Lord told me that we were in slavery; we were in bondage. For 27 years I have been praying, so I decided that this time I would stay. We had a lot of seminars [for the elections] and all-night prayer. We were praying about a lot of things in order that God's preference of government would be made.

'Everything you can think of was put in place to thwart God's preference. But every time these activities took place, it would be revealed and so we prayed against it. I had Muslims coming up to me saying, "We have prayed and we turned the results of the elections around. We are going to stay in power."

'And I said, "You are not going to, because God says He's going to put *His* preference in power. If you think *you* are the preference, we will see."

'So we prayed and at the end it wasn't easy. But now God has given us a president who is a born-again Christian, whose whole family is born-again. I want to thank God that, with prayer, God changes things. And He has changed this!

## Walk under God

'I'm appealing to you and anybody I meet, whenever you remember Sierra Leone, cry for mercy and pray for the President, Ernest Bai-Koroma. He's got a balanced cabinet, including Muslim clerics, but that is nothing to God when He wants to do what He wants to do. So I pray that you remember us for mercy, you remember that nation and that God will continue to use this man. In his swearing-in speech, the first thing he did was to thank God for putting him in power. He said he would walk under God as well as work with God, so that God might give him wisdom and understanding to rule the nation. That is what I am holding on to in my prayers for him. If he says he's going to walk under God, then he will have to work with God for Sierra Leone, so that the nation might be changed.

## For His Glory

'We're a wealthy nation, but if you go there, people are suffering. I am personally sponsoring people there in schools and colleges. The school that I went to, the old girls are sponsoring children there. For between £100 and £200 one can sponsor children with clothing and other essentials for a year. I do that in my own way. So this is the testimony. I want to give God all the glory that I am back in the UK.

'This is my land because I have lived here more than the place I was born in. So I've come back and I thank God for bringing me back. I just urge you all to remember Sierra Leone and ask for mercy because I know we are not in slavery any more. If you take the other two verses of our national anthem, the people who wrote it were really in tune with God as patriotic sons of Sierra Leone. But everything has changed in that land. We are saying that what God has started, He will turn around for His glory. Amen.'

What a powerful expression of faith in God!

Back home at St Mark's, we have the vision of growing *Deeper* with God, *Closer* to one another and *Further* out into society. We grow closer to each other in many ways, including through our smaller home groups and larger pastorate meetings, in which several home groups meet together. For those new to the church, both home groups and pastorates meet on the same night each week during term time. For those who are regulars, have you ever felt like skipping pastorate meetings? Well, here's the testimony of someone who used to feel that way, written in her own words:

*Pastorate Dodger*

*Conscientious and regular attenders of pastorate we were not. What changed? For myself, a new-found level of support and a depth of love. Colin and Marie Veitch head up a group of singles and couples with young children who have taken us to heart as parents of teenagers. We have come to enjoy the rhythm of our Tuesday evenings: the three home groups followed by a pastorate. This term we have had a visit from each member of the clergy in turn, telling us about himself and his passions. Great insights and available to other pastorates, Paul assures me.*

*Beverly Green*
*Pastorate Lover*

This 'pastorate dodging' changed into a success story because every part of the Body of Christ was working together and functioning as it's meant to.

# 14. A Stone at the Window

Paul Perkin asked Jesus into his life one summer Sunday evening while a student in Oxford.  He tells us here how it came about:

## Hiding Behind the Curtain

'I was brought up in a loving, stable and good home, but not a godly one, in the sense that we never went to church and the family Bible was very definitely in the bottom drawer! Jesus Christ barely ever crossed my mind, so I had no bias for or against Christianity (although to my continuing amusement and discomfort, I do remember the whole family hiding behind the curtain on the one occasion in my childhood when we saw the local vicar approaching the front door for a visit!).

## Theoretical Physics

'At Oxford I read theoretical physics — a wonderful world of universal origins and the Big Bang, of strange particles and antimatter, and of relativity and the GUT (Grand Unified Theory) or TOE (Theory of Everything)!  Whilst I never at the time saw this as pointing to the existence of God, I also realised that science could not claim to disprove God either.  Physics and metaphysics were not necessarily compatible, but they certainly weren't necessarily contradictory!

# A Stone

'That Sunday evening, after supper, I was settling down to read a book when there was a stone at my window (I was on the first floor). I opened the curtain, opened the window, and down below was a friend with whom I played sport. He asked, "Would you like to come to an informal seminar? There's a guest speaker, a friend of mine. He's going to talk about the meaning of the Christian faith for us today. It's in the seminar room across the quadrangle."

# Another Stone

'I replied that I was busy, closed the window, closed the curtain and went back to my book (actually, I was just reading a chapter before meeting an old school-friend in the pub). A minute later there was another stone at my window! Again, I opened the curtain and opened the window. Down below, my friend looked up and said to me, "I'll wait here until you come down!"

# Words that Made Sense

'It's not an approach I would recommend to others to invite a friend to hear about Christianity — but it worked with me! I followed him fifty yards across the quad to the seminar room and remember listening to a rather rambling talk peppered with stories rather like the ones in this book! What stood out, however, was that the speaker was talking about Jesus Christ as a living person and we could come to know Him in experience — talk to Him, and He talk to us. I remember hearing, for the first time in words that made sense to me, that this friendship with Christ was made possible because, on the cross when He died, He had cleared the way to restore relationship between God and mankind.

# A Little Booklet

'On the way out of the talk, I was handed a little booklet entitled *Becoming a Christian*. So I went back to my room, read the booklet in five minutes, and thought to myself, *This all looks reasonable — so that's that*. I knelt beside my bed (because that's the way I thought you said a prayer!) and I prayed the paragraph at the end of the booklet, inviting Jesus Christ to come into my life, to forgive me, to set me on the right path, and if He was real, to make Himself real to me. I must have repeated the request many times over, because by the time I'd finished, I was late in keeping my pre-arranged meeting at the pub. I raced off to find my school-friend, only to discover he'd gone, and I returned to my room rather disconsolate. But I did re-read the little booklet, just to see again what I had prayed.

## When He Comes... He Stays

'Little did I realise then that I had just made, in a rather casual fashion, a life-changing decision. It totally re-oriented my life's direction. I soon went on to ask the kind of questions that the Alpha Course is designed to answer — perhaps it would have been better if I'd asked them first! But I learnt in my own experience at the outset of my life of following Christ, that He can break into a person's life very simply and straightforwardly. It doesn't have to be a long pilgrimage and when He comes into a person's life, He stays.

## Another Invitation

'It also taught me not to despise 'the second stone'. On the receiving end, I wonder if I would have had a third chance to respond to the invitation to encounter Christ? And on the throwing end, I've tried not to give up when people show no immediate interest in the invitation to hear about Christ — they might be a bit like me, and all they need is another invitation!

## The Future

'As I prepared to leave university, my leanings towards the future gradually shifted. I had always assumed I would strive to be a career physicist, but now as a Christian, I increasingly wanted to be involved with young people in a teaching and learning environment. So first I became a physics teacher in a secondary school. I loved the energy and stimulation, and occasionally the exhilaration of the classroom. But I reflected on a slogan I'd picked up in my postgraduate education course: 'Teach John, not Latin!' In my case it crystallised into 'Teach

John, not physics', and soon afterwards 'Teach John the Christian Faith, not physics'. That was where my heart eventually lay, and although I've kept my love — and some reading of science — the transition from school-teaching to ordained ministry, teaching the faith, was a fairly smooth and logical one.

'My old school-friend became a Christian believer too, and he's now also a vicar; as is the friend who threw stones at my window — but that's another story (or two)!'

# 15. Supernatural and Miraculous

We had a prophecy conference here run by Streams Ministries in 2007. The St Mark's people who went on it were asked: Did any of you hear, see or sense something from God at the recent Art of Hearing God conference?  As editor, I'll be brave and go first:

## Dancing Lights

'One exercise we had to do involved sitting in a group of six.  Each person in turn was to listen for a word of encouragement from God for each of the others.  I sat with a group of five women, none of whom I knew. This helped me feel uninhibited to step out and take risks about what I might be hearing, seeing or sensing.  A picture, which I saw in my mind's eye very clearly for one lady, was of a few trees, in front of which were several dancing lights.  Her response was to burst into a Cheshire cat grin before I'd even finished!  To try to help make sense of the word of knowledge, I added that in the Bible trees can symbolise people.  I also suggested that lights can be a sign of angelic presence.  I then offered the interpretation that maybe God was saying she was going to be experiencing the supernatural and be used to lead others into that realm.  When I'd finished she said, "I'll tell you about the lights afterwards!"

'Much later that day, I caught up with her to find out what the word had meant to her.  The night before, this lady had been in her hotel room with two other conference attendees.  They had spent time praying and praising God still excited from a conference on God's glory, which they'd attended two weeks earlier.  Afterwards they went to bed and started to see lights in the room.  Surprised, they made sure that the curtains were properly closed so that there was no mistaking these lights for car headlights.  The lights kept dancing! Then other supernatural phenomena appeared.  She told me about seeing an angel's wing, an angel's face, and even the cloud of God's presence appearing in the room, apparently, like a fog.  It seems the Lord had given this lady a confirming word of what she had already started to experience.'

## A Beautiful Fragrance

Greet Oosterbeek replied, 'Yes, I did experience something special.  During the last session, I could smell a beautiful fragrance that filled the room. The smell reminded me of a boiled sweet that I know in the form of a pear drop, only the smell was much more beautiful.  As I left, I mentioned it to one of the speakers who replied that our Lord would speak to me like that.  This has left me feeling special, although I do not yet know what it means.'

## A Remarkable Intercessory Ministry

Caroline Hazell responded, 'A strange thing happened in the first exercise, where we had our eyes closed as we listened to God. As my unknown 'partner' approached and touched me on the shoulder, the picture I saw turned out to have been of her.  Only I did not realise it at first as it was a bit unclear, just a dark figure with what looked like straw round the neck, so I said I'd seen a scarecrow! In fact, she was a dark-skinned girl wearing black and a yellow, streaked scarf. We walked to Clapham Junction station together afterwards and she told me about her remarkable intercessory ministry, receiving through the Spirit names, pictures and situations otherwise unknown to her, into which she prays. One example: she foresaw a serious car crash in which a car fell over a bridge; she prayed and the driver survived, as she learned from news reports the next day. Her gift only came when she felt compelled one night to wake at 4 a.m. and start praying! (She no longer has to pray that early.)'

Now from hearing God to ways He answers us when we pray. Neil Smith shares first:

## 'A Really Nice Answer to Prayer'

'Because of my appearance and because I have difficulty walking (due to impaired balance and movement), when I go to bars and places where there's door staff, I frequently get stopped and hassled. I find it quite rude and offensive at times and I don't always respond in a godly way. That's something I'm really working on and praying about.

'A while back, I was going to a bar near Clapham Junction, meeting some people there. I was praying before I went that things would be all right. On my way there, I got stopped by a homeless guy who asked me for some money. I said, "No thanks, I don't really give out money but can I buy you something?"

'He said, "No, I don't need anything." So I walked on by.

'Then he called me back and he said, "Thank you, thanks very much. That's the perfect way to respond to a homeless person when they ask you for money. Thank you for taking the time to speak to me."

'I was really blessed by that response. I continued on my way and I was giving thanks to God for that, because it was so nice. Then I walked up to the bar and I was all relaxed. I just walked straight into the bar past the door staff with no hassle whatsoever. It was a really nice answer to prayer.'

And, last but not least, a testimony of another 'really nice answer to prayer' which James Ewins shared with us in February 2008, in case you missed it:

## 'Chances of... Conceiving... Miraculous'

'As many of you will know, I've had some very intensive chemotherapy in the last five years. The good news is: the doctors continue to say that I'm all clear, which is marvellous. But one of the consequences of having intensive chemo is that the doctors have confined the chances of me and Tiff conceiving another child to the miraculous. So I'm asking you to uphold us in prayer, as feeling very unworthy and very thankful — we're going for a 12-week scan!'

Paul commented, 'That is absolutely extraordinary!'

Six months later, Tiff was holding a very laid-back, twelve-day-old Florence, who was born on 19th August 2008. She's both a little sweetie and a miracle baby. Praise God!

From the supernatural to the miraculous, it's quite simply all part of God's glorious repertoire!

# 16. The Holy Spirit's Presence

Have you ever felt the presence of the Holy Spirit? Two people tell us what it felt like for them. First, Charlotte De Groot shares her amazing experience:

## 'I Thought I Was a Christian'

'Up to the age of 28 I thought I was a Christian. You know, I did all the right things: I believed in God; I believed in Jesus; I went to church; I believed the Bible was a true statement. I never read it, but I believed it. Then when I was 28 and heavily pregnant with my first child, Jennifer, I went and visited my sister down in Portsmouth. Rachel was a Christian and she wanted me to go to her church with her.  She was very nervous because it was a Pentecostal church and they were a lot more charismatic than a normal C of E church, which was what I'd been used to.

## Singing Worship Songs

'She prepared me for it and said it would be a bit more 'happy clappy' than I was accustomed to. It was, but I felt comfortable with it. Then they started singing worship songs. I felt self-conscious to start with. Gradually, I joined in and before I knew it, I was just totally and utterly wrapped up in the words I was singing and I started to sob. I was filled with joy and happiness; I felt peace; I felt alive and inside my tummy I could feel Jennifer dancing. She was meant to be head down so logic said she couldn't be, but I could feel these two little feet dancing to that music. As it turned out, she was a breach baby and she *was* actually dancing in my tummy! So the whole experience for me was absolutely amazing.

## 'How Inconvenient'

'Rachel found out about a church near to me and it happened to be St Mark's. I used to come on my own every week, as my husband, Andrew, was Roman Catholic, so he wasn't too keen on coming with me to a C of E church. Then one Sunday I woke up and I felt God telling me to dress up (St Mark's is quite casual) and put my make-up on. So I did. I came downstairs and Andrew said, "I'm going to look after the children today and I feel you should go to church and just relax." I don't know why. He'd never said that any other Sunday.

'So I came to church and it was packed due to a guest speaker. He gave a fantastic sermon and I remember being riveted by it. Then suddenly he stopped half way through it and he said, "I'm going to be really obedient now because God is telling me that someone in this place is going to come to Christ today." I remember thinking, *I wish you'd get on with your sermon. How inconvenient!* Then he said, "Can I ask that person to stand up?" As I was having these thoughts, I found myself standing up. I don't know how; I don't remember doing it. He said, "Would you come to the front." I went up and when I got there he said, "Are you willing to give your life to Christ today?"

'I said, "Yes!"

'He said, "Will you say the sinner's prayer with me? Will you ask forgiveness from God?" He was obviously going to say a prayer, so I gladly repeated it after him.

## Wonderful Feeling

'As I said those words, it felt like a cold, cold shower was going through my body and just washing me out clean. It was pushing down on my body and the same feeling I'd had the first time around was filling me up again with joy, happiness and peace. I started to cry. As this cold feeling got to the bottom of my toes, I felt like everything that was dirty and bad, everything I'd ever felt that was wrong, had just been taken away from me, as though every load had been taken off my shoulders. I was filled with this wonderful feeling of new life and I went back into the congregation.

'He continued with his sermon and at the end one of the staff came up and said, "Well, Charlotte, that was pretty amazing, wasn't it?!" Yes, but I couldn't put it into words so I quietly went home and didn't tell Andrew all day.

'It was only when I was ironing that night I said, "Something really weird happened to me today."

'Fortunately Andrew had been around a number of friends at school who were born-again Christians and he said, "Well, I think what happened there, Charlotte, is that you became a born-again Christian; you've just got a new life," and he explained it to me.'

## 'A Bit of a Loose Goose'

'My name is Rob Burrell and I recently had an experience that I found pretty profound and meaningful. I come from a standard Christian family, which in Zimbabwe means going once a week to church. At boarding school, I started to detest the Anglican Church because we had it rammed down our throats. I was the furthest thing from an effervescent, charismatic Christian and I've always felt rather awkward and embarrassed by the raising of hands and all that sort of stuff. I used to go to church by myself outside church services because I didn't subscribe to a lot of the liturgy, recall and response, and so on. So, I've been a bit of a loose goose for a couple of years [i.e. moved around, doing his own thing].

# 'I Needed Some Form of Proof'

'A couple of months after doing the Alpha Course, I'd also reached a point with God where I was looking for confirmation. I needed some form of proof and that proof was on my own terms because it was a condition that I'd made up myself. Then one Sunday I was struggling from a vicious hangover and I was in the least match-fit form for a church service! I didn't want to be there and I wanted the service to end. I was very tired and wasn't focusing on anything. I was sitting at the back and for some reason the singing was at the end of the service, after the sermon. The words started to come alive for me and I suddenly felt quite vulnerable. Then I realised I was about to cry and I felt this overwhelming sense of a warmth and a presence. It was quite unsettling, so I sat down.

# A Really Beautiful Experience

'As soon as I sat down, I started to sob uncontrollably. It was a feeling of relief. The spooky part about it all was that I felt this heat and pressure on the side of my jaws behind my face. I opened my eyes to check whether someone had come to hold my head, it was so real. At that moment it was very profound. The power was like someone was holding my face and looking straight at me and saying, "Here I am; I'm holding you; this is what you wanted but it's on My terms [i.e. God's]." None of it was on my terms.

'It completely floored me and it was so, so amazing. I liked getting away with the excuse of not having tangible proof for myself. I knew that this was the end of that because He had met me where I was, in His own way, through a really beautiful experience. With regard to prayer, I've never really known what it was like. But in that moment while I was in this dialogue, I knew what it meant to be in that state of communication. It was absolutely two-way. Now I'm coming to post-Alpha [a follow-up to the Alpha Course] and to regular services, because I don't want to lose what that meant to me.'

May God bless us all with the presence of His Holy Spirit and in ever greater measure!

# 17. Money

Every culture has a touchy subject. Money could be one of ours, but Beatrice Gbadebo isn't holding back:

## Tithes and Offerings

'Growing up as a child I was taught to tithe and fast from a very young age by my grandmother Lucy John, God bless her soul. Over the years I have treated God like a pay-as-you-go scheme regarding my tithes and offerings. For example, I would pay £20 per week all inclusive (tithes, offering and mission evangelism).

## Arrears on My Celestial Account

'I would often skip payments and started to 'owe' Him a lot of money, so my New Year's resolution was to clear all my debts with God. I came up with a decent amount in my eyes (though looking back now it may have been a bit on the light side). Anyway, on the first Sunday I tried to pay the arrears on my celestial account but by the time I'd finished filling in the gift envelope, the little bag at the back had vanished. So I said, "Devil get behind me!" and sent my daughter to give the envelope to the Pastor. I felt good and relieved.

## 'Breaking My Promise to God'

'A week later the final instalment was due and again the bag disappeared! I now decided that I would need £20 of the money and I could not be bothered to go to the cash point. I found the lady who keeps the bag and handed the offering to her myself [minus the £20]. After all, I had the children with me and their needs come first; I tried to justify why I was breaking my promise to God. I said I would pay Him back the following Sunday!

## About Accountability

'When I got home I noticed that there was mail waiting for me that I had not picked up from Saturday. So I opened it to find a letter from my solicitors informing me of a settlement for a compensation claim dating all the way back to 2000. It was for 150 times more than what I had put in for and they said they felt it should be a bit more! I was asked to give them my consent for this action. But it was never about the money, it was about accountability, so this would not happen to someone else! When Father God contends for you, that garment of shame is removed. He gave me beauty for ashes, strength for fear, gladness for mourning, and peace in despair. I felt so embarrassed.'

Beatrice wanted to share a verse from Matthew's Gospel which has significant meaning to her in the light of her experience: (Mat. 28:20) 'Teaching them to observe all things whatsoever I have commanded you: and, lo I am with you always, even unto the end of the world. Amen.' She ends on an enthusiastic, 'PRAISE GOD! HALLELUJAH! JESUS IS ALIVE!'

Our second testimony comes from Janice Whyne whom many of us know well from her work with CAP [Christians Against Poverty]. She herself has been greatly helped out of debt through their work. After leaving university in debt, she admits she then failed to take control of her finances in the way she might have done once she started work. She gives us a small insight into her former difficulties with money and how she experienced God's unexpected provision:

## Worried About Money

'A few years ago I was living in Leicester; I was having money worries and it was my birthday. Most people are happy on their birthday and I usually am, but on this particular birthday I was a bit sad because I was worried about money. In the evening I was going to be taken to dinner and a friend was paying, so that was fine. Another friend's mum was baking me a cake, so that was really great. But I knew that my friends would want to come back to my place

afterwards for a piece of cake and a cup of tea, and I had no tea-bags. I stood in my kitchen that afternoon talking to God and asked Him if I could afford to spend my last couple of pounds on tea-bags.

## Tea-bags

'Now, I'm not talking about your PG Tips or your Tetley (and I'm definitely not talking about Earl Grey, which I now love). I'm talking about the cheapest of cheap. Well, I went to dinner and I was having a good time, but in the back of my mind I just kept thinking about those tea bags — probably helped by the fact that I could see *Iceland* [the freezer supermarket chain] through the restaurant window. When the time came to leave, I got ready to cross the road to go over to *Iceland* and spend my last couple of pounds on tea-bags. But my friend wanted to show me the cake, so I went to his car and saw a beautiful cake. I made some comment but wasn't really concentrating as I was still preoccupied by the thought of the tea-bags.

## 'God Knows What We Need'

'Then he said, "And my mum sent these." He pulled out a clear bag, full of tea-bags! I nearly burst into tears. It's only stubborn pride that kept them in. No one in the world knew that I needed tea-bags except God. I thought, *Why would He care about such a small insignificant thing as one of these?* The answer is that He knew that — as crazy as it may seem — they were my greatest need at that time. In the Bible, it says that God knows what we need even before we ask it. In a way, I didn't actually ask God for it. I was just having a conversation with God, talking to Him, asking Him whether I could afford them. I was talking to my Father, my Provider, my All-Sufficient One and I was asking Him to be involved in my life, my everyday life. He saw my need and provided for it.

'That's what prayer — talking and listening to God — does; it says, "I want You to be involved." That day He was involved in such a beautiful way that, when I left Leicester four months later, I had tea-bags to give away.'

May God bless us all with much more than we could ask or imagine — enough to give away!

# 18. Drugs and Anger

We get an insight into a first-hand experience of the effect drugs can have and how God can step in.  Bob Peacock shares his story:

## Nothing, Despair, Hopelessness

'Puff [marijuana] was one of the worst drugs I could ever have got on to because I'm a thinker, so I used to sit and think for long periods of time.   Puff makes you chase endless thoughts round and you come up with nothing, despair, hopelessness.  That's what gradually happened.  I used more and more of it.   I was angry, but the drugs changed me and I became even angrier, more resentful and more volatile.

## Losing the Plot

'I used to pass St Mark's every day on my way to work over a period of about six months.  Then I got this strange urge to come to church one night.  I even got as far as looking at the window with the Alpha signs up saying: 'explore the meaning of life'.  But I carried on and forgot about it.  Three months later, I was walking past again and a voice said to me as clear as a bell, "Why don't you go to church?  What are you frightened of?  A big man like you!"

'I thought I was losing the plot!  I told the blokes at work and they said, "If you feel like going to church, why don't you?"  The last thing I thought these bricklayers would be telling me was to go to church!  I knew what they were like.  Ted, who was one of them, a Roman Catholic, said, "I go to church every Sunday.  Go!  You might enjoy it."  So I did — but not until I hit crisis point.

## A Stressful Day

'I came home from work one day and it had been another stressful day.  I was told to sort my son out.  I thought, *I don't need this stress when I come home.  Right, I'll sort him out once and for all.*  My son ran into his bedroom.  He got his feet down behind the door and his back up against the wardrobe.  I went to his door and I said "You've got two seconds to open that door or I'm going to break it down."  Well, he didn't open it, so I started punching the door.  I just kept punching and punching until there was a hole the size of a dustbin lid in the door.  But as I looked through the door, I saw the total abject terror on my son's face.  And it stopped me.

'I just stopped and told him to go out and give me time to calm down.  I smoked drugs all night long and stayed up thinking.  I had thoughts going through my mind like: *What sort of man is that who tries to kill his own son?  You don't deserve to live!  What sort of man are you?*  I decided in the morning that the best thing to do was to kill myself.  [Without going into details] the next morning, I had a mental breakdown.  I grabbed my coat and walked out of the house.

## 'I Was Going to Kill Myself'

'I was going to kill myself.  I didn't tell anyone about it; I was just going to do it.  [After thinking about the options] I decided, *Well I'll walk down to Battersea Rise.  The way they come down that hill, the buses are really mad sometimes.  I'll just walk out in front of one.  It'll have no chance because I'll just get under the wheels.*  So that's what I decided to do.  I came out, walked to the gate and God spoke to me the last time.  All He said was, "Go to church!"  I thought, *Church?*  I don't know what sort of help I thought I was going to get.  I walked down to the church and Natalie Kirk  [now Garratt, a former staff member] opened the door and said, "Can I help you?"

'I said, "Yeah, I want to speak to the vicar." I was crying. I don't know what she thought.

'She said, "The vicar is not here at the moment, but come in, I'll get someone to talk to you."

## Tears

'Natalie brought Rob Hooks [an American]. He came over and his first words were, "What's up buddy?" I thought, *Oh no... that's all I need!* But he came and took me into the old hall, sat there and said, "Just tell us what's wrong."

'So I started to tell him, for some reason. People kept coming in and I burst into tears. When people walked into the hall, I said, "Right, that's it. I'm off! I'm not standing here talking with people watching me crying!" I wanted to get away.

'Rob said, "Just stay there. You're all right. No one's looking at you." I kept telling him what was going on [in my life] and crying.

'Then he prayed for me and he put his hand on my shoulder. He didn't ask me if he could. I was going to punch him. He said, "Just let me pray for you." I can't really remember what he said — something about peace — but his last words to me as he finished were, "Look, why don't you come to church on Sunday? It might not be like when you were a kid." [Church had been awful as a kid, but how could he know?!] He said, "Come on Sunday, 10.30."

'So I said, "All right, thanks mate."

## 'I Gave My Life to Jesus'

'Anyway, I felt better after the first time I went to St Mark's, so I went again. And I kept coming. I met the boys from Stepping Stones [a Christian support and rehabilitation organization for ex-prisoners]. I could talk to them. They talked about doing the Alpha Course, so I did it and I gradually started learning more and more about Jesus.

'Mick Bow, one of the leaders, invited me round to his house. Mick just loved me and that had an effect on me. No one had bothered about me up till then. I shared a room with him at the Holy Spirit weekend away. I had decided to become a Christian, but the drugs got the better of me. I went and celebrated by taking far too many and made myself really ill. I felt so embarrassed at what I'd done. I knew I couldn't carry on like that anymore. On the following Wednesday at the next Alpha evening, I got hold of Mick during the coffee break and said I wanted to become a Christian. He prayed with me and that's how I gave my life to Jesus.

## Jesus is Lord!

'About six months after I'd said the prayer to become a Christian — and I must have said that prayer about 20 or 30 times in between, just to make sure the Lord heard me — I was reading a book about how to invite the Holy Spirit in. One night I had this dream: As I walked into a gymnasium, there was a neon light flashing JESUS IS LORD! JESUS IS LORD! There were all these strange people walking around, about 12 of them, all with long, black robes on. They came over to me and said, "Who are you?"

'"I'm Bob" I said.

'One of them said, "Why don't you come and sit down?"

'As I sat down I heard this voice saying, "So much anger; so much anger; so much anger." One of the men then crossed my arms across my chest and pushed me forward in the chair. All I heard was a voice saying, "Does the Lord ever do evil? Does the Lord ever do evil? So much anger! So much anger!" With that, this feeling started happening to me in my dream: it was like someone had put a fire over each foot and water started rushing through my body. But then I realised, it wasn't water it was wind — wind going through me faster and faster, so much so that it woke me up.

'For about 15 minutes after I woke up, it was still going! I kept saying, "Is that You Lord?" But ever since that time, I've felt calmer. It was as though the Lord had taken away my anger. I can control my anger better these days and I'm gradually getting freer. I don't react as much now.'

Knowing Jesus has totally changed Bob's life. When he first became a Christian, Bob read the Bible twice through in the first year and about 60 different Christian books. That's certainly hungering and thirsting after God, isn't it?!

# 19. On the Streets

How would you react if someone attacked you on the street out of the blue?  Alice Codner knows!  She tells her story here:

## Punched in the Face

'One night, while I was walking along with some friends, this random woman, whom I didn't know, punched me in the face!  She looked at me and was getting ready to do it again.  It suddenly flashed into my head the bit in the book *The Cross and the Switchblade* where the author [David Wilkerson] was about to be attacked and he said to the person, "Jesus loves you!"  So I said, "Jesus loves you!" to this woman and she paused and looked at me.  Then she ran off after my friend.

'In that time, I managed to grab a passer-by.  The woman came back and said, "What were you doing with my boyfriend?"  (There had been a guy following us.)

'So I said, "Well, actually, I believe in Jesus, so I'm not going to do anything with your boyfriend."  She stopped shouting and seemed to understand.  This gave enough time for the two guys who were standing by to come around me to protect me.  Then they called the police and she was taken away.  But that was amazing!  It was God looking after me.'

Tim Mayfield prayed for Alice that the Lord would restore her spirit and give her peace. Two weeks later Alice told me (the Editor) how she was feeling so much better. She has been completely fine ever since sharing her testimony, which was very good, she said, because she didn't want to become nervous. That sounds like Tim's prayer was answered. Thank You, Lord!

Jonathan Coad went out on the streets too, but reports a completely different experience:

## Bad Back Pain

'I'm a bit hesitant about this but I'll give it anyway. All my adult life I've suffered from quite bad back pain if I stand up for any length of time, like when I go to long gigs where you have to stand up, a sporting event or even a drinks party. I'm in such bad pain at the end of it I can hardly stand, which has got worse as I've grown older.

'Last month I was up at a friend's church in Birmingham. They'd decided to go out on the streets with that church and offer prayer for healing on the streets. Seriously brave! I thought, *Well, if the guys have got the guts to do that, I'm going to go along and support them*. Quick as a flash I found myself in the chair on the street saying that I had severe back pain if I stood up for any length of time (which is a problem if you're a bass player carrying a heavy five-string bass for a rehearsal and then a gig).

## Right Leg was Longer

'The guy pulled my legs out and said, "One of your legs is longer than the other." So I looked down slightly sceptically, but actually when you looked at them, one *was* longer than the other. My right leg was slightly longer than my left. I thought, *Well, I know what's going to happen now!* He said, "I'm going to pray." And I looked on as he prayed. And I really struggle with this. I find the whole healing issue very, very difficult theologically. But as far as I could work out, by the end of his prayer, both my legs were the same length. [After being prayed for Jonathan had felt, initially, as though he had something in the sole of his shoe as he stood on the leg which had been shorter.]

'All I can say is: This was about a month ago. I test it particularly when I go and watch my little boy play football, as I stand up for an hour when I do that. Now, I can't say the back pain has gone. All I can tell you is that it's now measurably less than it was when I stand up for a period of time.'

Now to end, something closer to home with Jules Springer sharing:

# Two Extremes

'A few weeks ago, Nick [Stott] was doing a sharing spot and I was thinking, *Oh, here we go, someone else to tell me about how amazing everything is with them and God, when for me it's straight, old, humdrum, day in day out, just the usual. It's always them, always them.* But I've had a time of learning and an opportunity to see some of the things which I tend to put on my scepticism and my cynicism to, when other people come and testify about the greatness of God.

'Just as in one of the songs we were singing about praising the Lord when it's absolutely fantastic or when things are the pits, I find that in the two extremes, I can be fantastic. When everything's hitting the fan you've got absolutely nothing else, and dependence [on God] comes easily. When things are brilliant, they're brilliant. But it's very much those in-between times, when you can pretty much do things in your own strength in just getting up, going to school, coming home — the everyday — and there's nothing godly in it as such.

# God in the Everyday

'Then I was having a monthly catch-up with my rugby dad and his friends. They get a green card [a permit] once a month from their partners and we go out for dinner and have a boys' evening. We were meeting them after work and I saw a guy sitting on the tube next to me flicking through Romans 5. I realised then just how much I compartmentalise God: in the morning for prayer, or in the evening for prayer, or in church on a Sunday. But recently there's been that character building, that learning about how God cares just as much when you're sitting on the tube waiting to get somewhere as when you're reading your Bible. So, in fact, I've been learning to really trust and depend on God and know God in the everyday.'

'God in my everyday, more so I pray; God be in everything, in every way!'

# 20. Following Jesus

These testimonies were first collected for our newsletters. As editor, it has been a privilege to put them together — to meet people I barely know and discover the reality of God in their lives. Sarah Raskino's testimony made people laugh when she gave it, but beyond the superficial fun of her story, you will see how Christ has come into her life and transformed her from the inside. Here is her story, in her own words:

## PG Tips

'I grew up in a Christian family in the north-east of England, by the sea. I was a good girl and I read my Bible, prayed and went to church every week. I did all the things Christians do. When I was 14 I went to a youth event in Newcastle with my youth group. The guy who was speaking was called Clive Calver and he was talking on the 'PG Tips'.

'One of the 'PG Tips' was 'Playing the Game' (of being a Christian). It made me really think, *Oh am I just playing the game? Am I really following Jesus? Or am I just doing all the outer things that Christians do?* That night changed my life for ever because I feel like I met God for the first time and I believe that's when His Holy Spirit came into my heart. My heart was pounding and all the things that I was very aware of before, seemed less important compared to suddenly being overwhelmed by how much God loved me. He loved me so much He sent His Son to die for me. That was just incredible and it felt really, really personal. That night was a special one that I'll never forget.

## Liberated

'About my job: I'm a bra technologist. I work for different lingerie companies, grading different sizes of bras for them. There are about 200 different patterns in one bra, so it's very complicated ... [*Much laughter in the background!*] Supposedly about 70% of women in the UK walk around wearing the wrong size, so they've got wires sticking in and straps pulling and it's all really uncomfortable. You need to go and get measured ... [*even more laughter in the background!*] by a professional and then they will give you the perfect-sized bra and you will just feel liberated forever! Now, without taking this analogy too far, being a Christian before I met God and experienced the Holy Spirit was a bit like walking around with a set of rules that didn't really fit. It was just religion and I didn't feel free or liberated.

## 'I Wanted to Do Things to Please God'

'After I experienced God, the focus of my life changed. Instead of me trying to tick all the boxes, do the right thing, be good and earn Brownie points, the focus was much more on wanting to know God and know more about the relationship with Him. Instead of doing a prayer slot, I just found myself talking to Him as I was walking along. When I read the Bible, instead of it being a duty, things seemed to jump out and speak to me personally. That was the difference. It was a bit like falling in love and I wanted to do things to please God, not because they were the right thing to do, but because I wanted Him to be proud of me. The things that had been really important before, like what my friends thought of me, were not as important compared to knowing how much God loved me and accepted me the way I was.

# The World of Fashion

'Since then my life has had its ups and downs like everyone else's. I went to college and sat on the fence a bit. I was really torn between the Christian world and the fashion world and all the things which that involved. All my Christian friends were speech therapists, occupational therapists, nurses and very helpful people and I thought, *What can I do in the world of fashion and design?*

'I worked for three or four years after college and then I discovered a project that was being set up in Bombay which was training women from the slums and the red light area in tailoring so that they could have an option of another lifestyle. So I went out to India and helped set up a Fairtrade company. This was 15 years ago, so we were pioneers. It was not like today where it's everywhere!

'The people at work thought I was completely crazy giving up my job and life in London (half the church probably thought so too!) but I really felt like God had told me what to do and I had to follow Him. In my life, whenever I have managed to put God first, He's always blessed me loads — loads more than I could imagine — and made things all right for me. When I went to India I met Luke and we got married and we lived there for six years doing that work together.

A Trainee at the Jacob's Well        Slum dwelling in Bombay (Mumbai)

# The Way God Sees People

'In India I learned something about the way God sees people differently from the way that I had. Instead of feeling sorry for the people who didn't have as much as we did, I realised that a lot of people in poor countries are much richer spiritually than we are. We have a bank account we can go to if we need something and they have to rely totally on God and pray with faith. They often see their prayers answered very quickly because of the way they do that. I realised that it doesn't really matter to God what I'm wearing and what kind of car I drive (either way), because He's only looking at my heart and my attitude.

'When I left India eight years ago I really felt that God was saying to me, "It's not what you do, it's who you are that matters to Me". That's been a real challenge, and still is, because I like to be busy doing lots of things. I feel like God wants me to just be still enough to get to know Him, be in a relationship with Him and actually hear what *He* wants me to do, rather than spending my life running round doing loads of other things. I think it's easy to live life on the physical and emotional level and a lot of my years have passed by just doing that. But, when I open myself up to God, I get on to a spiritual level with Him as well — and that's when the most exciting things happen in my life.'

Wonderful! Isn't what Sarah says so true?! That is certainly when the most exciting things happen in my life. Praise God!

# 21. Divorce

Welcome! Many of you will know Joe and Sue Gavin from the excellent meals they cook for various courses at St Mark's, like the Alpha Course and The Marriage Course. They've been married for 21 years, but they've had a stormy past. Joe shares a bit of what's gone on and how, once he came to Christ, submitting to the Lord has made the difference in their lives.

## Divorce Papers

'When I was in prison Sue and I split up because of my crime. Sue sent me all the divorce papers but God said to me, "Don't get divorced. It's not My way." He showed me the scriptures in the Bible where it says  about divorce and He said, "I'll bring the pair of you back together again."

'I said to God, "No way!"'

'He said, "Yes, I will bring you both back together again."'

'So I said to God, "The woman hates me, really does hate me for what I've done. I've destroyed her life…" and God said, "Believe in me, and I'll bring you back together again."

## 'God, Can You Help Me?'

'When I came out of prison, I got in touch with my sister again. I hadn't really kept up much contact with her. She said to me, "Phone your mum."

'I said, "Well, I don't get on with my mum. She hates me."

'Again she said, "Get in contact with your mum."

'So I did and my mum turned round and said, "Oh Sue's trying to get hold of you!"

'I said to my mum, "Have you got a phone number or an address for Sue?"

'She said, "No, I haven't, I don't know where it is. It's somewhere. I'll look tomorrow."

'This was a Saturday night and she said she'd look for it on the Sunday. I hung the phone up and thought, *I wonder what the best way of doing this is,* and I handed it over to God. I was praying and said, "God, can you help me with my mum's eyes, guide her hands to find the phone number — whatever's necessary? Amen."

'As I said amen my phone rang and it was my mum! She said, "I've just found the phone number." So I phoned Sue up. I had a nickname for her and when I phoned her, she couldn't believe it was me. She actually burst into tears because she'd thought that I didn't want to know her anymore. On Sue's side, she'd just had this number going round and round in her head, so she decided to dial that number and that's how she got in contact with my mum!

## Back Together

'Later I said, "Come up to St Mark's. You'll love the people up there." Sue was absolutely terrified of coming because she'd had a couple of bad experiences with church. I laid my hands on her and prayed for her down in the High Street. She came and, apparently, Sue was speaking to people here and they'd say, "I know you already."

'"How do you know me already?" she'd ask.

'She was told, "All Joe talks about is you!" So we got back together and we did a double whammy here. We got baptised and we retook our marriage vows on the same night. That was about three or four years ago. We're still together and it's a lot, lot better this time!

## The Word of the Lord Stands Forever

'Sue had a bit of a problem and she ended up in hospital. I said some really cruel things to her about it. I was reading a book by John Stott on bird watching, which is about spending quiet time with God. So I went out bird watching and God said to me, "You were so wrong, it was so evil what you said to your wife." He wasn't pleased with it and He told me that I had to make amends for it – basically repent. I went back and took a big bunch of flowers and said sorry to her and apologised to God as well. He's helped us a lot! I started here [at St Mark's] with nothing, just as a pot washer, and now I'm heading up the cooking on various courses. I firmly believe what it says in the Bible in Isaiah 40:8 – *The word of the Lord stands forever*.

## Giving up Smoking

'At last year's women's weekend away I brought Sue up here and put her on a bus to get the coach from St Mark's. I went home, threw all the tobacco down the toilet, emptied all my ashtrays and said, "That's it, God; it's in Your hands now." A year later I'm still not smoking. I just gave it  up. I tried to give up smoking a long time ago. When I phoned Sue up on the women's weekend away and said I'd given up smoking, she didn't want to come home because I was the most evil person going [due to the withdrawal symptoms]. Whenever I gave up smoking, I wrecked the place. I'd smash things; I'd throw things around because of the nicotine coming out of my system.

'When I told Sue she got terrified. She's thinking, *I don't want to go home! There's not going to be a flat left!* It gives me another goal to work towards, but it's the best thing I've done. You don't realise it, but the few quid you spend every day, it soon mounts up.

You might as well put it on a bonfire and burn it when you think of the damage you're doing to your insides. And to the people around you as well – Sue suffers with bronchitis, so my smoking was affecting her. When you're around Christians you become very aware that you smell like an ashtray. With the general public you don't mind, but when you're around Christians – that's what got me; I felt really terrible because I'd stink like an ashtray. I'd get women at church coming up to me and saying, "Hello Joe" and giving me a kiss on the cheek and I'd think, *Don't come near me! I smell.*

## Temple of the Holy Spirit

'I get cravings; that's natural, but God's behind me. What does it say in the Bible? It says your body is a temple of the Holy Spirit. Well, you wouldn't smoke to pollute your temple. That's what I keep saying. If I get cravings, I just keep saying that verse and fight against them. And the beautiful thing about it is: I worked out smoking costs me over £900 a year. The first year alone I saved £500 and bought myself a laptop out of it just through giving up smoking. That would have been £900 I'd have burned! At the end of the day, if you really want to do it, you can. With God's help it can be done. You've got to know that God's standing with you, that you're not doing it alone. I gave up smoking just like that and feel a lot better for it.'

May Joe's testimony be an encouragement to anyone else trying to give up smoking!

# 22. Hearing God

Welcome! Do you ever feel challenged by God? Well, when God challenges us, it's always for the best. Perhaps you will relate to Sarah Mawle as she shares her feelings with us:

## 'Peace Be With You'

'This year has been one of those funny old years where nothing has been awful (far from it) and nothing has been great. Yet all year I've been wishing I was on permanent holiday, travelling the world, away from the routine of life. The annoying thing is, since I started feeling like this, I've also known that this is not about to happen imminently. A number of times when I've asked God, "Where should we go?" there has been silence.

'But I've been really challenged by the 'Jesus in John' series [evening services, Spring term 2008], in particular by the words "Peace be with you!" (John 20:19, 21), which Jesus gave the disciples when He met them in the upper room, and the word *shalom* [the Hebrew word for *peace*] meaning: life at its best. I was challenged that this is what God wants me to know — not when I'm on holiday or travelling the world, but a wholeness and tranquillity in *all* of life.

# When God Blesses Us...

'The penultimate talk was about the abundant blessing that Jesus delivers — it was the story of the disciples out fishing when Jesus met them on the beach. The disciples had been out fishing all night, but had caught nothing. Then Jesus told them to throw the net over the other side of the boat and that time the net was filled to overflowing! I was reminded that when God blesses us, it's abundant.

# ...It Will Be Abundant

'I've been holding on to these two words for the last three weeks. I was really challenged to believe them for myself. I felt like Jesus was saying, "You've got to believe these promises; change your way of thinking." So, rather than thinking, *Oh I wish I was in South America or Europe or somewhere on a beach*, I've chosen to believe that this is where God wants me, that He wants me to have peace (instead of always wishing I was somewhere else) and that when He blesses me it's going to be abundant.

'Although nothing has changed [in circumstances], these words have really lifted my spirits; they've renewed my joy and enthusiasm. So I want to encourage everyone to accept God's promises and choose to believe them. Sometimes it takes a conscious effort — at least, it does for me! But I know He *will* bless us and, when the blessing comes, it *will* be abundant. So I'm looking forward to it!'

Next, Mimi Sheldon tells us how the prophecy seminar at the church weekend away in May 2008 convinced her that God really does speak to us!

# One Minute

'I wasn't very sure what prophecy was all about; it turned out that prophecy is about having a word or a picture from God for somebody else to strengthen, comfort and encourage them. So that made it a lot clearer to me. Anne Coles was running the workshop and she was brilliant — a very wise, calm and humble woman. I liked her.

She split us up into groups of four. I knew one girl in my group a bit and didn't know the other two women at all. We had one minute to say, "God, what's Your word for this person?" We would all do the same for that one person.

'The one minute meant your mind had no time to wander. It was incredible! Every time, in our group of four, two of us had exactly the same picture or word for that person, not knowing anything about them. For example, I had a picture of an apple for one person and someone else had a picture of an apple orchard for that same person. Two other people both had a picture of a very sturdy front door for me. I thought, *This is real material evidence from God that I haven't ever felt before.* It was amazing! We're not quite sure what the words all mean yet. Some of them are clear; some aren't. But we've taken each other's email addresses and we're going to email each other as soon as those words become clear in our lives.'

Still on the subject of how God can speak, Rachel Larlee recounts an experience of hers:

## Shocked

'One Sunday I was walking to church and went past my neighbour's house. I heard a rustling and saw some movement just below their window. I looked and I saw what I thought was a twig moving, quite a thick twig. When I looked more closely, I saw it was actually the tail of a rat. Then I saw a nose and some ears; I was a bit shocked, to say the least! I knocked on the neighbour's door but there was nobody there. So I went back to my house and got [husband] Dave to have a look. He said there was nothing really that we could do apart from write a note and put it through the neighbour's letterbox to say what we'd seen.

'The rat was nestling behind a brick. There were lots of leaves quite high up, probably about 30 cm from the ground, dead leaves and twigs and old bricks. Anyway, I was on my way to church and I was freaked out by this and it made me feel a bit sick. But I didn't really think anything of it at the time.

## A Real Warning

'We'd just come back from a holiday in Florida where Dave and I had spent all the time praying and waiting on God. We'd spent time sorting through some of the rubbish in our lives that was blocking God and we'd come back with a clean slate.

'During the worship at church that Sunday, I was reminded of the rat. I felt the Lord say to me that the rat was only there at that particular house because of all the rubbish and the leaves. It had chosen that house because they hadn't bothered to clear things out of the way. If I didn't make sure that, as rubbish came into my life, I cleared it out, then that's what was going to happen. It would be like a rat in my life again.

'I felt the Lord say that I should make sure I clear out all the anger, all of the frustration, any unforgiveness and any resentment or jealousy that would come — and anything that would squash my faith. I sensed that it was a real warning to make sure there was no room in my heart for any rubbish, and to do my best to sweep it away in order to keep a clean heart for Him.'

Yes Lord, give us a pure heart and help us keep any 'rats' out of our lives!

# 23. Stormy Seas

John Hall, a retired clergyman, attends the St Mark's nine o'clock service. Here he shares with us his inspiring story of how he came into his calling:

## 'When I Grow Up I'm Going to Be a Sailor'

'When the war finished, a lot of people came back home in uniform. I had uncles who were in the navy and they looked very smart in their uniforms. Well, I thought, *When I grow up I'm going to be a sailor.* I had difficulties with learning because of dyslexia, which nobody knew about in those days; they just thought I was thick! When I was 13 I went to nautical college, the Nautical Boulevard, with a view to training in Navigation Seamanship to be a ship's officer.

## A Horrendous Storm

'I was on a ship in Norway with a cargo of iron ore. Now, iron ore is very, very heavy stuff so you don't need a lot of it in the ship to make it go down to its load lines, but it does mean that when the ship goes out, it's very unstable. There's a tremendous weight in the bottom and when the storms come, the top of the ship moves but the bottom doesn't... so you get this pendulum effect.

'We set sail to go to Philadelphia in Baltimore and, in the middle of the Atlantic, we ran into a horrendous storm. In a storm like that you can't really do very much except keep the ship's head to wind. The ship not only rolls from side to side but it pitches and tosses. When it goes down into the water, the water comes on to the foredeck of the ship so there's a huge wall of water; as the ship goes down it's like it's going down below and then it suddenly comes up and all the water rushes down the foredeck and just smashes against the bridge-house so the whole ship shakes.

## 'I Thought We Were Going to Die!'

'Well, we were like that for ten days and I was on watch from eight o'clock until noon and eight o'clock at night until midnight. It was a terrifying experience. I stood on the bridge of the ship and all I could do was make sure the bow kept into the waves and wasn't amidships to it as it would have capsized. I thought we were going to die!

'I'd been brought up as an altar boy server. I'd been confirmed; I'd been baptised; been a Crusader — all that kind of thing. But I didn't really know God. Now, I looked up at the bridge of the ship and I prayed a prayer, "O God — if there *is* a God, and You get me out of this — I'm going to clean up my life and I'm going to change things. I'm not going to go on as I've been doing." When you're on a ship like that, there's nothing you can do; the lifeboats are smashed; people are picked up like matchsticks; the ferocity of this storm was unbelievable. We couldn't get to Philadelphia but we limped into St John's,

Newfoundland. I don't know how long we were there getting the ship repaired. The damage was terrible.

## 'What Is a Christian?'

'We were in there for a Sunday. The wireless operator and the Second Officer said to me, "John, we're going to church. Would you like to come?" So I thought, *Yeah, I did make a promise that if You got me out of this, I'd do something about it.* I was really trying to take it seriously and that began a search for God. When I had finished my term on the ship, I came back to do my examinations. I found a group of people who talked as if they knew God personally. It was different: they read their Bibles and they prayed. It was so different from the high church. I felt much more at home in the high church practices than I did in the evangelical wing, but eventually I asked them, "What is a Christian?" I'd been confirmed by the Archbishop of York. You can't get any higher than that! But I came to see that by grace you're saved through faith, that it's a gift of God and not of works.

## 'I Heard a Voice'

'One very dark, foggy night I was lying in my bed and I thought, *God what do You want me to do with my life?* And I heard a voice, "I want you to be a preacher."

'Well, I didn't really take that very seriously. I was building up to the examinations which were quite stiff. I thought I should talk to the rector of the church and he said, "I think, John, you should take it seriously." It was a bit of a laugh really, you know: *Preacher! There's no way* I'm *going to get up and preach!* He wrote a letter to Dr. Coggan, who was the principal of St John's Hall at Lingfield.

'So I went down to see Dr. Coggan and I told him about what had happened. He said, "John, you should take it seriously."

'Days later I got a letter from the Bishop saying that I could go to a selection conference. So I went and then a week or so later I got a letter back saying, "You've been selected for further training." Well, that really put the cat among the pigeons! I wrote back to Dr. Coggan and explained things. He offered me a place at college starting in the new term." So I went back to naval college and did my exams.

## 'God Moves in Mysterious Ways'

'I got through my exams! It was incredible because of my learning difficulty as they were really hard. The shipping firm offered me a ship and I said, "Well, actually I'm going to be ordained in the Church of England." I couldn't believe I was saying it! Then I got my call-up papers. Everybody had to do two years' National Service. They put me in the Royal Engineers. Believe it or not, the Royal Engineers had a fleet of ships and I got a job instructing in Navigation Seamanship. While I was in the army I met some Christian Brethren (Open Brethren). I thought, *Brethren? I'm going to be ordained in the Church of England! Oh dear!*

'But they loved the Lord and they said, "Oh, are you going to be ordained? Will you take a Bible study?" Well, I couldn't have told you where the Acts of the Apostles were in the Bible! I hadn't a clue!

And then they said, "Give your testimony. We're having a local open-air campaign." *Give my testimony? What's that?!* But I was able to get grounded. You see, you can't go to church when you're at sea, so it was really a preparation. I thought it was a frustration! It was amazing how God worked. God moves in mysterious ways!'

John finished his stint in the Royal Engineers and started at the London College of Divinity. Eventually, despite his dyslexia, he went on to become Rev. Dr. John Hall, and was Rector of Tooting for 27 years! John's is a testimony of how, if God has called you, He will enable you. It's surely an inspiration to us all in one way or another. To God be the glory!

# 24. Weekday Moments

Are you someone who finds themselves at a loss when it comes to witnessing at work? If you are, then you'll identify with Stephen Denby who shares how he broke through:

## Denied

'Every Friday at work, I have a scintillating conversation with a colleague of mine. I say to him, "Have a good weekend," and he will say to me, "Yeah, you have a good weekend too." We're both men, you see, so we don't have much to say to each other! Then I say to him, "Well, what are you up to at the weekend?"

'He usually says something like, "I'm going to go and watch my local football club. What are you up to?"

'Well, the Friday before Folkestone [church weekend away] we had our usual conversation and he said to me, "What are you up to at the weekend?"

'I said [rather sheepishly], "I'm, er, going down ... to see some friends ... on the south coast. [*Much laughter from the congregation!*] I didn't laugh at the time. I did just think, and had this voice in my head saying: *You have just denied your Lord. You've just said, "I do not know Him."*

## A Chance to Redeem Myself

'I had this voice in my head all weekend. There were seminars, including one about work. It was really beating in on my head. I did think, *Actually I've got a chance to redeem myself here* because I've started doing Prison Alpha on Tuesday nights and I knew I had to leave work early to do this. So I prepared myself and thought, *Come on! Think about what you're doing!* I had to leave work at five o'clock and thought very carefully about it. I prayed about it. I even had verses of the Bible lined up that I was going to quote at him, if he asked me about prisoners!

'So, when I was leaving, he said, "Oh you're off early. Where are you going?" And I just told him. I told him what I was doing, talked about the church's ministry; I told him about the rehabilitation for prisoners and why we were doing it. Well, he was really, really interested!

## How Effective...

'The next day he asked me about it and I told him all about it. I don't know where he stands with God, but he seems to be someone who has a heart for it and I felt redeemed in a way with that. I suppose what I'm trying to say is: maybe for those of us who work in professions which aren't the sort of professions people naturally associate with Christianity (in the City or lawyers or whatever), if you think 10 per cent as much about how you witness at work and the strategy for the day, events you've got coming up and opportunities you're going to have to witness to people as much as you think about the next presentation, the next *PowerPoint* presentation, the next brief, the next policy paper that you're writing, then how effective could some of us be?!'

From Stephen's city environment to a less glamorous area of work, Neil Smith tells us how he handled a rather blunt question one morning:

# 'On My Way to Work...'

'I was on my way to work in Brixton when a prostitute approached me and she said, "Do you want sex?"

'I said, "No, thank you." [*Much laughter from the congregation!*]

'Then she said, "Well, can you give me some money, please?"

'I said, "What do you want? I'll buy it for you."

'She said, "I was mugged last night and all my money was taken from me. Could you buy me a train ticket to where I'm staying?"

'So I went and bought her a rail ticket and then she said, "Can you buy me something to eat?" So I bought her something to eat.

'We were just coming out of the shop and she turned round to me and said, "Are you sure you don't want sex?"

'I said, "You're worth more than that! God loves you."

'And she looked at me and said, "I know."

'I don't know why she said that, whether people had told her lots of times before or whether it actually touched her somewhere inside, but I hugged her and said, "Take care of yourself! I've got to go to work." She went on her way.

'But I want to encourage you, because I find it really difficult to pray when I'm by myself at home and virtually never have a 'quiet time' (you know, like we're supposed to do). [*More laughter!*] I just want to say that whatever state you're in, as long as your heart is towards God and you're open, He can use you.'

Helen Johnson was prompted by Neil's story (shortly before she was due to be away over the summer of 2008) to share how God spoke to her about a challenging subject:

## Beautiful Child

'I'm currently studying at the School of Hygiene and Tropical Medicine and as part of my course I have to do a long project over the summer before I finish, to do some research preferably in the developing world. I've known this all year so that I could plan it. Last autumn I was travelling on the Underground when I saw an advert for a charity. It was a child sponsorship charity with a really beautiful child in

Sierra Leone and where you could change this child's life. I thought, *Oh you know, I really could; I could do my project in Sierra Leone or somewhere where I could work with children.*

## Project

'I'm really interested in maths so it's a maths-based project. All the doors that opened up meant that the project I *am* going to be working on is not with children at all. It's with male sex workers in Bangalore. These are men who service men. I found that quite challenging but lots of opportunities opened up to that. I was travelling on the Underground again recently, as I do every day, and I saw the same advert, with the same child and the same charity. A little bit of me thought, *I'm not going to be working with those beautiful children. I'm going to be working with these male sex workers in India.* But I really felt God say to me, "You *are*, you're going to be working with *My* beautiful children." I found that really challenging and reaffirming.'

No matter what our status, age, sex or ethnic background, we're *all* God's beautiful children!

# Exploring Further

We are ordinary people who have been surprised and delighted by what God can do in our lives, especially in answer to prayer.

Maybe one or two of these stories have answered a question you had about God's reality. Perhaps they have left you curious and raised new questions about Christianity.

Whatever the case, if you would like to explore the Christian faith further, we would recommend the Alpha Course. Details of your local course can be found at alpha.org).

You are always welcome at St Mark's (details of our Alpha Course, and church services, can be found at www.stmarks-battersea.org.uk).

If you want to explore the idea of knowing Jesus further, you might also like to read Nicky Gumbel's short *Why Jesus?* or a longer book by C.S. Lewis entitled *Mere Christianity*.

Perhaps you have sensed that these stories are relevant to you and that God could be real in your own life. Maybe you feel ready to take the next step. Jesus Christ made it possible for us to have a relationship with God as a heavenly Father, by dying in our place on the cross. If you would like to know Jesus, wherever you are at this moment, we would invite you simply to pray the words on the following page:

*Lord Jesus, I want to know You personally too; please help my unbelief. Thank You for dying for me on the cross. Please forgive me for all that I've done that has offended You and that has hurt other people, especially the hidden wrong attitudes and unloving thoughts, words and actions [name them if you can]. I want to change my old ways. I ask You to come into my life. I'm taking a step of faith and I give You my life. Open my eyes to You and teach me Your perfect way. Open my heart to Your love. Open my world to the joy of Your friendship. Amen.*

If you said that prayer with sincerity, then you have begun a relationship with God and it needs to be developed. If this book was a gift, then tell the person who gave it to you that you said this prayer. Keep building your faith by reading a passage from a Bible in contemporary language, (for example *The Message* Bible or the *Good News* Bible) with the help of some notes to guide you (such as *Everyday with Jesus* by CWR or *Daily Bread* by Scripture Union). And be sure to join with other believers in worship and learning.

We believe the testimonies in this book, thrilling as they are, barely scratch the surface of what is possible in a life with Jesus. May you join us in the adventure of experiencing a real faith in Him. God bless                                                                    you!